T0070217

Facial Hair and Cleavage Culture

FACIAL HAIR AND CLEAVAGE CULTURE

STAN ROBINSON

Algora Publishing
New York

Library of Congress Cataloging-in-Publication Data —

Raber, J. O.
Famous, but no children / J.O. Raber.
    pages cm
Includes bibliographical references.
ISBN 978-1-62894-042-8 (soft cover: alk. paper) — ISBN 978-1-62894-043-
5 (hard cover: alk. paper) — ISBN 978-1-62894-044-2 (e) 1. Childfree choice. 2.
Men. 3. Women. I. Title.
    HQ734.R117 2014
    306.87—dc23
                                    2014001045

Printed in the United States

TABLE OF CONTENTS

Preface

I have 95 years' experience of the opportunities and obstacles facing Americans. Right now, I can say that America is bleeding, with no hero who will come to our rescue.

The solution lies with the citizenry. The first requirement is that America must learn to Cope. That is the only path to winning. Needless to say COPING is scarcely known in American society. People who know how to COPE are those with simply savvy on how to observe and assess the pros and cons of a situation and decide how to behave, through self-awareness. It is the only path to win and stop the downfall of our inadequate culture. There is a major battle in order to achieve the return of America the Beautiful and all that is promised to our populace. Our nation is the only place on the planet that affirms the right of its citizenry to the pursuit of happiness, and it has been seen as a bastion of liberty where all citizens are welcome to strive to achieve the American Dream.

I experienced America the Beautiful shortly after World War II, when the country seemed to be the embodiment of a true powerful democracy based on righteousness. I have kept my eye on this national and personal self-definition until my present state, which I call 95 years young. I am confident that Freedom and Liberty were the medicine that allowed me to reach this happy age.

The solution lies neither in food nor exercise, but maintaining in the spirit of America the Beautiful while COPING in a righteous manner. Unfortunately the latter is recognized by quite a small portion of our citizenry. We are now dealing with a negative environment which requires everyone wishing to have a successful, fulfilling life to adopt a particular *opposing* lifestyle that will enable them to find peace and happiness while avoiding tension. I clearly delineate the process of COPING under the negative state of America the Ugly. The next ten chapters show how that is achievable.

The contemporary culture which I have analyzed extensively reflects the fumbling, floundering state of America. It is a negative, multi-movement culture that is taking shape among the population. Their response to the changing times is totally inadequate since they are unaware of the Reality of their discomfort. (I'm going to tell you shortly what I mean by Reality.) Consequently in the recognized culture there are many defensive movements, for the most part totally inadequate yet serving some level of satisfaction to some segment of the masses. In the long run there is no recognizable improvement and as the enterprise worsens, the culture takes on unsatisfactory superficial characteristics, providing only minimal peace and happiness.

I am ready to serve America at a critical moment in history. I see this opportunity in the same manner that I did for World War II where I volunteered in the United States Navy spending over two years on the high seas which was totally filled with explosives/mines, bombs in infested waters. I wish to make the American Dream once again available to our people in order to provide true peace and happiness to our citizens.

We are at a serious moment in history. Many historians have demonstrated clearly that a number of cultures have reached a level of complications whereby there was a severe cultural change. America has moved into that stature. Needless to say there is a way to win and COPING is the answer. Consequently the populace must gain the necessary insights regarding coping, all of which will be explained as we move along.

I have written this treatise with a privileged, unbiased innocence that allows me to pierce the prevailing mystery of the creation of America the Ugly. The Facial Hair and Cleavage Culture are a sad derivative created by America the Ugly. To be 95 years young and possess the vigor of a 60-year-old is the result of the state of my inner self, a state that would provide the wisdom and ability to make America beautiful again, if enough people can learn how to pull themselves out of the mess and re-orient themselves. Our citizens must learn the process necessary in order to make the difference. The inept ugly state of America can be altered by a level of COPING that protects the people by gaining the necessary insights that I am about to provide. I wish to aid our country once again, as wholeheartedly as I did in 1943.

As you read, I hope you'll be inspired to join the struggle to abate and vanquish the enemy that is represented by the Facial Hair and Cleavage Culture. Let's return America to being the country of the lifetime pursuit of happiness. I am positive that the objective is attainable by sharing my knowledge and experience that will take us to the Promised Land. We must avoid this false new culture, seeking and drawing forth elements of the true American culture to build our country up again into a nation that can be proud of its values and achievements. Learn to Cope and Win.

CHAPTER 1. THE PLAYING FIELD

Let me describe my own personal experience of the American Dream. By including my bio, I can set the scene for our exploration of America past, present, and potential for the future, while sharing what I've learned about how to get the most out of life by learning how to fulfil your own version of the American Dream.

Primarily in this chapter I will provide comments of the playing field I encountered when I began life. You'll soon see that disciplining oneself to hold to the right values and perspectives will enable you to make the most of your experiences, helping you to cope and survive while moving on through a positive lifetime experience and longevity.

The Beginning

Born in 1922, Saco, Maine, population 9000. Parents Lithuanian immigrants. They did not rise above their backward, provincial European experience. Mother would not learn to read or write. Both mother and sister developed severe mental problems due to hardships. Father was non communicative.

Central heating did not exist in our house, with winter temperatures running 10 to 40 degrees below zero. Hot water was heated on the kitchen stove. The only heated room was the kitchen. Bathroom bathing was not possible from Thanksgiving to Easter. Parental guidance was nonexistent. Conflict was the basis for personal interaction. Mother and sister fought physically and frequently. When people came to visit, mother pulled down the shades and locked the doors. I felt sorry for my folks and felt pity in my heart. I was determined to find the proper solutions which would lead me to longevity and happiness.

Childhood

I had only one toy during this entire period, a small metal tractor. This forced opportunity for inner creatively. I played with the ants on the sidewalk, building tunnels and hills for the ants to climb, etc. They were most cooperative. Eventually I earned enough money to buy a sled, ice skates and a fishing pole. Fishing was forbidden; therefore I had to hide my equipment in the porch foundation.

I started my first business at the age of twelve. In those days there were no supermarkets, but instead there were specialty stores such as: fruit, groceries, cheese, coffee and eggs. Also the products were shipped in wooden crates and when empty, they were discarded at the rear of the store. I built a wooden wheelbarrow and collected the crates. I disassembled them, cut the pieces to proper length, and sold them as kindling for 15 cents a bushel. Kindling was required in order to start a fire in the kitchen stove. Gas or electric stoves to my recollection were not available. I often earned 75 cents a day, always banking 90 percent and the remainder went in my pocket. I followed this banking principle throughout a great portion of my life. It seems appropriate to list at this point, some of my occupations from ages 13 to 16 as follows:

1. Age 13, Roustabout - Carnival
2. Age 14, Golf Caddy
3. Age 15, Salesman Mobile Fruit Wagon
4. Age 16, Toolmaker (at this age) I was also working as a professional musician.

High School

Thornton Academy is a private school. It was 200 years old

and located in my hometown. Local tax payers could achieve free status for their children, and it was the way I entered the Academy. At the end of my first gym class, the teacher warned us that he wanted us to take a shower before returning to other classes. I asked a student at my side "what is a shower"? He showed me, and I can assure you, from then on, I never missed a gym class. It was heaven.

I graduated from Thornton in a College Scientific Curriculum in 1941. I served as business manager of my class. At graduation time, I announced that we had raised so much money that my office would host the entire class at a dinner dance at the Cascade Lodge. In 2006, sixty-five years later, I was elevated to the title Distinguished Alumnus, presented with a trophy and requested to address the graduating class. As a result of the vetting process I was invited to submit credentials and comments on experience which was matched against those of other alumni.

College

In the fall of 1941, I left my job as a tool maker (while playing nights in music) to matriculate at Syracuse University to study engineering. At that time I had only saved enough money for one semester, however I earned a 50 percent scholarship during the first semester, and therefore was safe for one year. However, I was surprised to learn that I had to pay for my own books, and I didn't have the 35 dollars to do so. In this dilemma, I decided to seek advice at the campus nondenominational chapel. The minister listened to my story and came back from his office with the money saying; "pay me when you get it."

When I arrived at the campus with my saxophone, I was totally unknown. I went to the college employment office and accepted three jobs. I was a housekeeper at several houses, an elevator operator in the hospital, and lastly, a very special endeavor as follows: Once a week on Friday evening, I donned rubber clothing, grabbed my shovel, and entered the hospital incinerator where among other things were the remains of various body parts. My task was to shovel the material into a truck.

In addition to pay, I was given a weekly meal ticket for

the cafeteria. During the summer vacation after my freshman year, I was selected to become an engineering intern at the Caborundum Company, Niagara Falls, New York. With that summer pay and with my 50 percent scholarship, I was able to enter my second year.

Music And Military

However, I eventually joined the Syracuse Musician Union and commenced playing nights in various parts of upstate New York, while going to school during the days.

December 7, 1941 came about, when the Japanese attacked Pearl Harbor and the US entered the war in the Pacific. By the end of my sophomore year, I felt the need to join the conflict of World War II. The draft board told me to stay at school and earn an engineering degree, which was more valuable to the war effort, but I felt I could not stay behind while others were fighting. I gave up my deferment and joined the US Navy.

My last night as a civilian was spent playing at a country club, where there were approximately 400 dancers. The leader called up One O'Clock Jump. The arrangement started with a piano solo followed by a sax solo, which was mine. When I was finished, the leader signaled to take another solo and he did so approximately 15 times. There were no dancers, only listeners at the front of the stage. I really got my "kicks" that night before leaving civilian life.

I spent my total service on missions on the high seas as well as various training sessions in the US Navy serving in both the Atlantic and the Pacific campaigns.

A couple of anecdotes are worth recording for posterity. On one occasion on our ship there was a mysterious group called The Seven Marauders. They were apparently dominated by an impulse to search for insane pleasure. They would surround an individual in an isolated location and give him a beating or subject him to torture. One day while sitting on the fan tail (the end of the ship), by myself and washing my clothes, I saw seven sailors approaching me in a semicircle.

I quickly turned around, picked up a large iron wrench, and facing the group with determination I said, O.K., the first two are dead, let's get started, and I waved the piece of iron. Fortunately there were no starters, they melted away, never to confront me again.

The second anecdote again of interest on the unknown events in the Navy is as follows. As quartermaster, I was in charge of the bridge and the crew there in. One of the sailors ignored the rule never to raise a hand to another sailor. He attacked me from the rear and I made short work of him. However, he tried again one day to beat up the leader. This time I threw him down two flights of metal stairs. The anticipation was that he would be dead on arrival. Unfortunately that did not happen, but I was never bothered again. My crew nicknamed me "The Bear."

Returning To Civilian Life

I came home to Maine and found because of stress, I could not stay in the house. I often think that the problem was that the house was not rolling with the ocean waves like a ship and created an aura of a fixed land-bound environment. I left my home and traveled as a hobo all over Eastern Canada and New England for six months.

During this period for several weeks, I worked as a woodsman on a sportsman fishing reservation in the White Mountains of New Hampshire. Working in an environment in the wilds was a wonderful therapy. We slept in the bunk house on the side of the mountain, and my sleep was often disturbed by drunken hobos (homeless men) who wanted to beat me up. I am proud to say they made the mistake. I learned a short poem from a man of the road as follows:

I bummed around from coast to coast
And had no placed to stop
I'm just like the eagles wing
And always on the flop

I had many interesting experiences as a hobo, observing the world from such a low vantage point. It is astounding how this research can be advantageous. I certainly learned to stay vigilant, even after the war.

Returning To Syracuse

After six months on the road I was ready to return to a normal life, hence to Syracuse University to achieve a bachelor engineering on the GI Bill of Rights. At this point, I had been out of music for four years and no longer was competitive. I went to work as a stevedore in the railroad yards. This return occurred in late 1947. It was at this point that I had walked into a jewelry store and I saw a young lady working as a clerk. The result was that I fell in love unknowingly when, I had no intention of doing so. I made all of my primary moves on the lady ending in her telling me to get lost. Approximately six months later we were engaged, and six months later, we were married. This occurred around the time I received my bachelor degree and landed my first job as a junior engineer with a major pharmaceutical company. I was promoted to chief engineer in three years. This was the start of life as a husband and professional.

Family

Lois and I had 67 years of bliss. She passed away on May 14, 2015. Our three offspring and several grandchildren all developed successful lives and established themselves in their professions. Our third child graduated as an electrical engineer from University of Pennsylvania and was selected as one of five top graduates in the country; he was given a complete fellowship, whereby he graduated from Stanford with a masters. However, in 1989 Leslie succumbed to leukemia at the age of 26. Such a tragedy would certainly rock anyone's boat, but Lois and I always sought to hold a positive approach to life and her presence was the apex of my life. Nothing has ever been more important in my life than that lady.

Professional Life

In over 43 years span, I worked in the fields of pharmaceuticals, textiles, plastics, and personal items. This has been a constant path of growth, and I retired as an International Vice President for a major international corporation. My work took me to sixty countries. Under my direction were the International Export

Division, International Technical Operations, Worldwide Productivity Office, and The Travel Bureau. I joined this company in 1962 as chief industrial engineer, retiring in 1991.

During my entire professional career, I have placed great importance on advanced education, professional experiences, as well as literary research. Early in my career I recognized the need to broaden my engineering capacity and earned several degrees, all in night school with 100% scholarships.

First I went to night school at Union College in Schenectady, New York, to prepare for the extensive testing to achieve Licensed Professional Engineering status. I accomplished this in 1959 in Albany, New York, having passed the boards in Civil, Mechanical, Chemical, Electrical, and Industrial Engineering status. I later received my Masters in Engineering from Rensselaer Polytechnic Institute in Troy, New York, while serving on the teaching staff in the School of Management. During this same period, I created the School of Management at the Troy New York Community College while serving in professional capacities day time. Finally I achieved my Doctorate at Rensselaer Polytechnic Institute in Troy, New York, in the field of management and psychology. Additionally I have had nine books published in management and technology.

Leadership

I am a born leader and have a strong desire for responsibility. Leadership is mostly decision-making, and therefore the fundamentals of decision theory are a constant part of my awareness. A thumbnail sample is as follows: (1) Facts, (2) Probability, (3) Intuition.

As soon as you are faced with a situation, first search out the (1) facts in the case, even if only a few milliseconds are available. Move as soon as possible to item number (2), probability. While only a partial list of the facts may be available, you can start to get a sense of things by assigning probabilities on the occurrence to the unknowns. And finally, if there is no other solution, you have to gamble on your (3) intuition. This approach can be executed in milliseconds.

Needless to say, facts are necessary to develop the most

accurate decisions, and getting the facts requires the leader to maintain the proper composure throughout. It can be hard to stay calm and thoughtful when events challenge our emotions and trigger impulsive reactions.

I have interacted with individuals from almost all major cultures of the world, and I have lectured in many countries, always applying leadership capabilities. Since there can be danger associated with travel to some overseas countries, my staff and I trained in karate for approximately one year. That turned out to be a blessing.

We also participated in programs to raise our awareness of surveillance, defensive driving and kidnapping. In my own experience, I was attacked on six occasions by hoodlums with the intent to take my money. I am proud to say that their attempts were unsuccessful.

The nuances of leadership have served me well in the factory, executive row, with unions and at home. Here's one story from a manufacturing installation. It was my practice to inspect the entire facility on Friday afternoons. I usually skipped the ladies' restroom, for obvious reasons. However, on this particular day, I made arrangements see it. To my amazement, this area had never been overhauled since the original construction of the building.

After chastising my staff, I instructed them to immediately tear out the existing facility and rebuild it to the standard of my personal restroom, i.e., blue wall tile and floor, with matching fixtures. I obviously became the champion of the large packaging department staff with the ladies.

Lifestyle

When I reached the age of 40, I found, like most people, that my energy level was decreasing. I immediately entered into extended literary research regarding health. A great deal of the literature is not research, per se, but the opinions of various practitioners.

I concluded as follows; pesticides, growth hormones et al are poisonous to the human. Exercise is essential. Lois and I went totally organic and I remain so to this day. Experience indicates that this type of diet has innumerable advantages. Additionally, I installed a gym in our basement, and at the age of 50 I was able to press 250 lbs and as a general exercise, curl 150 lbs ten times.

Lois had a personal trainer and worked out five days a week. At age 88, I was still capable of running a one-mile warm-up as part of my regular workout. This lifestyle speaks to my vigor at 95 years of life.

Music And Other Interests

Next to my wife, music is my love. I spend my quiet moments writing poetry, actually song lyrics. I have finished a of poetry, and as a patriotic endeavor I have written a song titled "A Fresh Breath Of Freedom," which has been published. Obviously in our country the subject of freedom is no longer a conscious thought, but is taken for granted. It was my objective to create a suitable song that could serve to bring back the subject of freedom to a proper level of awareness. Songs have been used to activate soldiers, audiences and lovers to name a few. It seems logical that we can achieve a formidable contribution to our nation which is highly in need of an injection. Additionally I am now a member of The Academy of American Poets and have a group of my poems displayed at an Anthology in the state of Maine.

I have also published nine books, dealing with topics ranging from the divorce mania to "Leadership for the Non College Person."

Additionally, I would like to add that I was appointed a member of Mr. Trump's Presidential Advisory Board. I have been working with him since the election. He sent me a free ticket to the inauguration stating, "We did this together, you must attend." Then I received an invitation to have dinner with him at Trump Tower recently. As a veteran and patriot, I have put my heart into the values our country represents, namely the right and the opportunity to achieve as much as one honestly can, and I believe Mr. Trump is our "Fresh Breath of Freedom" aiming to push back against the encroaching "new values".

In my three endeavors (author, poet and composer), I am satisfied with my movement towards a successful status. When I achieve full public acclaim, then the final chapter of my life story will be titled: "Self-Actualization."

I have a PhD in Management and Psychology, and I have devoted 43 years to leading thousands of individuals in COPING and finally success. All of this, I wish to share now with our troubled Americans.

I began by presenting my life history as an example of reaching for — and attaining — The American Dream for several reasons: first, to illustrate that it is possible and to define the route to the American Dream; secondly I wish to share with my readers all that I have studied and my experiences in order to teach the art of COPING. This particular important knowledge will enable the troubled citizen to identify a personal solution to overcoming a problematic environment.

The only way to win over the Facial Hair and Cleavage Culture is to take my offerings as serious material. The American Republic is now operating in a new world where the old ways no longer guarantee national success. The major solution is good leadership in The White House.

Needless to say, I reached the state of being 95 Years Young entirely as a result of the manner in which I have lived and coped. It is important to keep in mind, as you construct each day of your life, that soon you'll be looking back on your life's experience, especially when you reach your declining years. The objective is to live in a manner that is heavily based on how successfully you have interacted with others.

Furthermore an extremely important aid over time is how you utilize your self-awareness. You must consciously behave wisely every day of your life and be motivated to find happiness within yourself and others.

Positive behavior is a great aid to your wellbeing. Frankly, that is one of the major themes of this entire treatise. I have been through just about the entire life cycle and have faced obstacles that needed to be overcome. I have faced sadness which was unplanned. In addition I have achieved many important professional objectives so that at age 95 I can rest in a state of personal comfort and satisfaction. In fact having lived my American Dream in which I am immersed, I would be pleased to hold everything as it is to infinity. Most important with my resultant wisdom overtime I can help others.

One subject to discuss is important to young people. Someone recently began promoting the attractive idea of having "the government" (that is, the taxpayers) offer free tuition; the younger generation would be most gracious in accepting the offer. However, they already have free tuition available, if you wish to take a side step. From the day that you enter High School, you should plan to be diligent and achieve qualifications for scholarships at the best colleges you can reach. I speak from experience since I received my bachelors on the GI Bill of Rights then my qualification for Professional Engineering (PE), all the way through Masters in Engineering and PhD in Management and Psychology, on 100% scholarships. From beginning to end I did not pay any tuition. Simply I did not have it.

The only decision is to plan your level of diligence and I can attest that it is by no means that much of a hardship while developing one's self-esteem. This subject is a matter obtainable through the American Dream in a very appropriate experience. I may point out that from beginning to end of my advanced education I accumulated 50% A's and 50 % B's, while working days as an executive. My motivation relates sincerely to my desire to be part of the American Dream. When you reach your reclining years it is a great boost to your personage to look back over your lifetime with comfort, pride and self satisfaction.

I consider myself a patriot, a contributor to society, an important family leader and, superimposed over my entire participation in life, is my citizenship in the USA. Consequently at age 21, I put my life on the line in World War II. And last but not least I have made it a priority to develop a constant high level of self-awareness to identify the righteous way. This state provides me with the ability to constantly find the righteous decision and behave accordingly. I am not claiming to be religious. The word righteous means the following: good, virtuous, upright and decent. The latter is the number one path to follow in order to find a way to peace and happiness. Above all, to stand in this position one must have the capability and motivation to help others. All in the vein of helping others and being a contribution, one finds happiness in a world that generally has not risen very well to this state.

Self-absorption and the absence of a drive to help further the general good is why so many people fail to achieve fulfillment. This is a shortcoming that each of us can only overcome on our own.

So, that's the basic playing field and the desirable environment for achieving peace and happiness and the benefits they bring.

I always strived to find what works and what does not. I best summarize my emotional history as follows. I have been hired and fired, promoted and penalized, criticized and rewarded, lauded, complimented, and I have both prevailed and failed. In general, I've met all the challenges that must be overcome. As a frame of reference throughout my trek through life, I have always relied on all the positives that I relate to the basic requirements of COPING with the complexities of the Playing Field. We must find the righteous path in all matters which allow us to discern the Reality leading to the American Dream.

The average life expectancy of Americans born this year is about 79 years. I am sixteen years ahead of the game, and most of all, I am enjoying my "Gifted Visit." The fundamental goal of this treatise is to explain what makes the difference. In a simplified statement, it is *the way I have lived.*

Chapter 2 will discuss general areas that are the obvious bases for achieving peace and happiness and the American Dream. I hope to achieve the status of being the oldest living World War II warrior, and to share with others what I've learned about life during this unusually long period of "study." The most singular critical value I happily record is Positivism. With a positive outlook at the forefront all this time, my 95 years have been most satisfying.

This attitude is particularly needed while overcoming the negative culture prevailing in America today. In the chapters to come, we'll have a discussion about successfully COPING with a negative culture and a negative environment for self-development. My own life history shows that the American Dream can be attained, even in immigrant families with few advantages. Preparedness for COPING under contrary conditions enables a person to function well even on the negative playing field.

CHAPTER 2. TODAY'S CULTURE DEFINED

It's time to establish the nature of America's New Culture and to recognize its negative effects. Then, by learning about COPING, we'll see how it's possible to change the scene and bring comfort and understanding to the those around us, as well as uncovering critical solutions to this dilemma.

We will provide the nature of this treatment clearly while describing the value of interrupting the path of devastation. As a society and as individuals, we are seriously challenged by the sad state of the world. However in COPING there is a strong possibility to change things for the better.

Circumstances around the globe have changed dramatically since the post-war era. Still cruising on its sense of hands-down victory, the US needs to adapt its mindset and its approach to other nations. Yet the US is somewhat inept, strained and in need of guidance. COPING begins with AWARENESS and a sound sense of REALITY, and this book will provide ideas on all three concepts.

America is experiencing its full share of an unpleasant "state of the union." At one time we could speak with satisfaction about our "social cohesion," but these days society is overwhelmed by events demonstrating that we are being divided, splintered and set against each other. Every day, scenes of hate, rancor, and deceit are witnessed on the streets, in business, at school, at every level of government and among rank-and-file citizens, eradicating the possibility of achieving togetherness.

This unfortunate environment is constantly in play and severely affects peace and happiness. Unfortunately the present unawareness and suitable response is totally ineffective while eliminating encouragement to peace and happiness. Avoidance is a negative stance and will never bring us success. The current state is a negative preoccupation and a path to failure.

Therefore we have a societal result that I have labeled "The Facial Hair And Cleavage Culture." We will deal with this phenomenon in this chapter "The Culture Defined."

Leadership is also a pre-requisite for societal success. For several decades, we have suffered with the lack of competence in managing our country. How can we move forward as a nation when, for instance, the atmosphere of obstruction rather than cooperation contributes to the negative characteristics we seen in today's culture. That "culture" has several segments that need complete exposure and treatment. These are listed as follows.

1. The Phenomenon of the Culture
2. The Promotion of Fear and the Militarization of the US
3. Facial Hair and Cleavage
4. Political Supposition Leadership
5. The overwhelming Threat of Excessive Immigration
6. The Unlawful Sanctuary Cities
7. The Deficit

The Phenomenon Of The New Culture

Alfred W. McCoy is a professor of history at the University of Wisconsin-Madison. He and Tom Engelhardt, author of several books and creator of the blog "tomdispatch.com," have recently recorded important material regarding the effect of the New Culture. They observe that the question is how to arrange a soft landing for America if there is a wake up in the populace. They suggest that if it faces the problem squarely, the United States may continue as a global super power. But under the current conditions there is too much unwarranted rancor, and an almost automatic resort to violence instead of thoughtful discussion of differences. Peace and happiness are difficult to attain under such circumstances.

Budget Deficits

There is one important element that they did not mention in their analysis. Few commentators care to admit we have a $21 trillion deficit, and that's just the federal deficit. Add in the states that are going bankrupt, counties, and municipalities.

The courage and savvy to overcome major obstacles requires tightening up in our managerial process. Additionally, we are hampered by the corruption in politics, the lack of willingness of Government to be more positive and the outright refusal to cooperate with our elected president on goals he has stated.

As the political temperature rises, we also see domestic unrest. It is important for the population to comprehend that the removal of the New Culture does not mean that America will shrivel up and disappear. As other countries advance and the wheels of history turn, we are seeing our power diminish from all points of view and our global status inevitably will return toward that of being an average country, no matter what. But dividing the nation and opposing our own elected leadership is the quickest route to failure.

Finally we have commenced under our new President. Unfortunately there is a prevailing state of insecurity among the populace and it is only increasing.

The Facial Hair And Cleavage

A careful examination of our problem clearly delineates an unusual internal culture that is quite distinct and motivated. We will discuss how this superficial culture came about. Even if you haven't consciously noticed these changes, once we list some of its features I'm sure you'll agree that this culture exists. Most people unwittingly accept these ugly developments as "just another day." Yet I have observed that the culture itself is the cause of their subconscious insecurity.

The culture provides an unconscious distraction on the whole problematic situation. There's no sign that people are concerned with seeking out the reality behind what's going on. When I describe the elements, this phenomenon will be clear and comprehensible.

America is insecure at various levels, which is certainly evidence of a threatening condition. However, most people seem uncertain, no, completely mystified as to where this threat really lies. Furthermore, many aspects of the culture are designed to tie us up in further self-absorption, to isolate us from each other and make genuine communication impossible, and to distract us from Reality.

The following is an itemized list describing some of the various behavior patterns which I have identified as demonstrative of the Facial Hair and Cleavage Culture. Think about them in relation to my previous systematic comments regarding the basic result of distraction from individual Reality.

1. Men refrain from shaving. I have asked them why? They don't know. Some use a trimmer, which adds neatness, and others don't care at all. Therefore the Facial Hair habit is a new highly-utilized popular change to the male's visage — and it is not necessarily an improvement. Whether the attribute noted is in fact simply the avoidance of shaving is questionable. One could argue that the condition does not provide a clear sensitive contributing motive and is totally unknown. Another possible motivator is masculine vanity. But overall, it reflects a state of casting off reality and mimicking others in order to create a false feeling of belonging and security.

2. While not shaving their beard, there is widespread fashion of men shaving their hair and boldly flaunting boldness. Is that a form of hiding racial differences by mutilating everyone's head?

3. Ladies increasingly show a proclivity to display their cleavage, or the mid-drift, whether they're entertainers on stage or seemingly thoughtful characters anchoring the TV news, presenting themselves as serious professionals or merely as private individuals. Why open the upper portion of their garments when they want to be appreciated as competent decision-makers rather than for their anatomy?

In terms of numbers, this ranges from 1 percent exposure to

50 percent exposure of the flesh. This habit is of rather recent origin and is quite unnecessary. It threatens self-esteem. The ladies are beautiful without the new fashion. However, the gain (if any) is the same as for men who go around with facial hair. It makes them think they're fitting in to some new trend, they're part of it, they "belong."

4. Marching demonstrations seem to be more frequent. Demonstrating is part of a democracy; however, because of the state of the nation, violence often occurs, running all the way from fist fighting to destroying buildings. The technique has become well-known at least since the 1960s, whereby members of the groups opposing the demonstrators will seemingly join in, infiltrate the marchers, then unleash a wave of violence and destruction that will discredit the original group. This violence, whether it comes from the demonstrators or from anti-demonstrators, only serves to increase our personal concern.

5. The design of the new hotpants getting ever closer to bikini-on-the-street has taken a new thrust whereby the buttocks are to be exposed. This is a shift that started in 1988; however, it seems to be reaching its apex recently. This category of design originated in Brazil.

6. Untucked is a creative word that tells you to desist from tucking in your shirt and this "fashion" also applies to the females. This trend, like others that demonstrate an unwillingness to make the least effort, appeared recently and has taken off like wildfire. Once again it offers false security under the assumption that it is a sign of belonging to a group, namely, the up-to-date, self-confident, cool guys who don't care about you or what you think.

7. Tattoos and Piercing are popular, and not just among teenagers. There are some people who have tattoos over their entire body. This trend has multiplied many times in recent years. Once again, this is just a continuing diversion from the identification of unpleasant reality. Medics call this Body Mutilation and say that it is connected with sadness.

7. Ladies' hairstyles have lost their luster. There seems to be nothing more than one style for all. Nothing more elaborate than a few curls is ever seen. Most young women, and many older ones, can't be bothered to do more than a simple part in the middle, with the hair hanging. This is flattering to approximately none of them. There are some minor individual touches such as one side is behind the ear. The result is minimal creativity, reduced challenge and a diversion from the courage to show a little individuality. Or, like most of the trends I'm pointing out, it means "I don't care about you or what you think."

8. Dancing used to be a sensitive and artistic pastime that succeeded best when we paid attention to our partners in a gentle give-and-take. It was a pleasure, and it played a role in getting a couple comfortable with each other. It encouraged peace, solitude and quietude. However, it requires a bit of effort to learn such dance techniques; and you have to care enough to develop the skill.

As popular music has become less musical and more aggressive, this type of dancing, where the focus was on one's partner, has been replaced by individuals, often with no partner in sight, or by simple displays and stage shows. Hip Hop and such dancing play no role in getting to know each other but rather encourage us to concentrate on our own performance. It further isolates us rather than bringing us together. Rap, and most modern popular music, does the same. In fact, if you listen to the lyrics, they are more likely to be driving wedges between people than calling for "all the world to sing." And who wants to even watch musicians dressed in crude and ugly outfits? They are projecting a loud message: We don't care. We don't care what you think of us, we don't care about you at all; we only care about ourselves.

9. Debasement Of Entertainment. I can no longer go to the movies, since there is little offered that is not negative entertainment. I cannot accept violence and killings as entertaining. Hollywood is centered in a financial-return mentality, come what may. People have been trained to expect

violence and cheap visceral stimulation, in other words a negation of human values, in their entertainment. Do you carry this violent training with you into your life after the movie? How can you not? Certainly peace and tranquility is not the objective. Murder insanity no doubt is the objective.

Unfortunately many entertainers are given to using four letter words while on stage. This apparently is acceptable and entertaining to a great portion of the populace. Needless to say I am out of synchronization with so many features of our negative culture. This problem has been created which causes undesirable effects to the subject of Togetherness.

10. Negative Codes Of Behavior. These are the effects of the negative codes of behavior that currently place our country in a constant state of tension. I am totally unaccustomed to the negative state of our present culture. How does this affect my normal codes of behavior? I refuse to alter or downgrade my standards. Thus, I'm limited to a small number of TV stations, as I seek to avoid the disrespect modeled on so many channels.

10. Shortly after the presidential election, a Congresswoman said Trump should be assassinated. Doesn't that sound like treason? Doesn't it amount to a rejection of our democratic process? Trump won the election. And yet the Congresswoman is still in office.

11. Immigration and sanctuary cities set up in opposition to the national will (as expressed by electing Trump), are a sapping our budget and dividing the country further. Until we take care of our own citizens born right here, we have no business even hinting that we would give a free ride to immigrants. This only encourages more people to leave their homes and come to ours. Sadly, the truth is that we cannot provide for them all, and it is already abundantly clear that sanctuary cities have more crime than others.

12. Drug and alcohol abuse continue to go up, among all segments of our society. That is not a sign of a people who feel fulfilled and it is not a sign of a people who know how to build a

better life for themselves, let alone others. Cop killing is a daily event. Murder has become a cultural travesty which includes children killing children.

13. The Washington Post has published an article that states that the Pledge of Allegiance is a bigotry statement. Those who encourage this kind of thinking are fracturing our society, when they should be working to forge a sense of shared history and shared qualities as human beings, shared responsibility for our country today, and a shared future. But thy only care about themselves.

14. Background music in the past during commercials was appropriate and pleasing. Now we have drums beating plus bells and whistles. In fact usually this approach is a distraction. Perhaps it reduces the cost of producing the ad, while reducing our ability to take in what is being said, so that we are easily and cheaply influenced and cannot rationally ponder the presentation. Another way to increase corporate profitability.

15. Sexual Harrasment. A great number of prominent politicians and business people, television anchors, Hollywood executives and others have been prosecuted in the past few years for sexual misconduct of subordinates, colleagues, even strangers, right up to raping children and running child prostitution rings. These are people with a lot of lawyers, personal security, and the ability to pay victims to keep quiet, so the fact that some have actually been caught tells us this is a very big iceberg. Sexual addiction and abjectly amoral behavior at the top indicates a very sick society.

16. Natural Disasters. Wild fires and hurricanes are creating havoc. People are losing their homes and finding their lives ruined. At the same time, there has been a kind of "storm warning culture" propagated over the last generation, adding to everyone's insecurity. Maybe this is going to be the big one; maybe it will change course or go up in a haze. The announcements and warnings are made in a tone of voice that is enough to give everyone nightmares.

There has also been a trend to dollarizing these events. It all boils down to how much money was lost, what was the cost of clean-up, how much insurance rates will rise. Again, the toll on our fellow human beings is no longer the focus.

17. Immigration And Open Borders. Last but not least, we are currently bombarded with the idea that allowing unlimited and unaccountable immigration would somehow be good for our country. Well, I suppose it sounds generous, and apparently many people suppose it would do no harm. But as I've said, what we suppose and what the facts show are quite different. This topic deserves a chapter of its own, in Chapter 3.

18. The Deficit. The national debt is over $21 trillion as of present. Incompetent business capability and poor decision making for several decades is the fundamental cause. Bankruptcy is a potential threat.

19. Congress. Congress is no longer a swamp it is a sewer. I am not sure that the public understands that Congress has a different work schedule than the citizenry. Most people work 250 days per year; Congress is officially in session just 120 days a year.

They have other privileges, too. They do not participate in the same healthcare plan as the populace. They purchase a separate plan made available by the DC Health Link. Additionally there are funds available that can be used for a wide variety of vaguely defined purposes, meaning they can be tapped in case a congressperson needs legal advice or needs to incentivize someone not to report harassment. This means the congress has little day-to-day motivation to improve the conditions in which we live: these conditions don't affect them.

20. The media cares more about ratings than honest reporting. They create fake news.

21. Students walk out of the classroom to demonstrate against matters they don't even understand.

22. Our national murder rate is beyond sanity.

23. The relationship between police and the citizens is completely broken. Policemen are no longer respected and they are hunted. At the same time, they no longer respect citizens, and frequently they shoot to kill when there is absolutely no need to do so.

24. Peace and tranquility are scarce. People have forgotten that it is the responsibility of each one of us to behave in a way that encourages cordial relations, and divorce is now 50 percent.

Supposition Strategy In Politics

A supposition is a belief held without proof, something you accept as true without forethought. What is not explained in this definition is the introduction of bias, which can influence our beliefs in highly negative ways. However we must deal with this total phenomenon as is. So therefore we will provide some examples. In so doing it is important to comprehend the unfortunate negative activity.

One relatively recent example of how the supposition strategy negatively affects our society came from President Obama. He presented us with Obamacare, hailed as a new healthcare insurance program for the whole population. The bill was under consideration for 25 days in a row, the second longest in history, tying up Congress. Yet most of the provisions in the final bill were negotiated behind closed doors, and there was in the end little opportunity for the Congress or the public to find out what was actually in the text until after it was signed and approved. Unfortunately, it has turned out to be a disaster. The important issue is that the overall cooperation was outstanding to such a degree that Mrs. Pelosi, Speaker of the House of Representatives made a statement: "We have to sign it to find out what's in it." In other words, they had to agree on the text, based only on what they supposed might be in it.

The Facial Hair and Cleavage Culture, I believe, is the result of subconscious insecurity derived from all the above factors and many more. That's why we have such a burning need to learn how to cope.

You can readily see how this strategy only magnifies the already stressful results among the masses. My purpose in demonstrating this strategy is to point out how insecure and inconsiderate so much of the public activity is cast upon our citizens and its acceleration of substandard tension. The result is that this creates unhappiness among the citizenry and simply accelerates the problem whereby Coping must come to bear.

Conclusion

These are some of the debilitating characteristics of The New Culture This incredibly dangerous state of affairs must be brought under control by those in authority, while at the same time the increasingly authoritarian state needs to find ways to reduce the violence and stop trammeling our rights to free expression and freedom of thought. If we are not allowed to say that a man is not a woman, and if it considered a crime of hate speech to indicate which person we mean by referring to salient factual characteristics such as skin color, religious affiliation, or place of origin, we have lost the right to even think objectively. If we cannot think straight, and we cannot be creative, we'll be going down very quickly.

CHAPTER 3. THE THREAT OF IMMIGRATION

The issue of illegal immigration places a burden on the entire United States, and it is a problem that is yet is unsolved. The best way to commence describing and analyzing the problem is to print several paragraphs of current research from The Fiscal Burden of Illegal Immigration on United States Taxpayers.*

Illegal immigration to the U.S. costs federal, state and local taxpayers a staggering net cost of $116 billion a year – an increase of some $16 billion compared to previous estimates – according to a new study released by the Federation for American Immigration Reform (FAIR). The study is the most comprehensive to date on the cost to federal, state and local taxpayers of the nation's 12.5 million illegal immigrants and their 4.2 million children as well.

The report, "The Fiscal Burden of Illegal Immigration on United States Taxpayers," examines the cost of illegal immigration through a detailed analysis of federal, state and local programs that are available to the nation's illegal immigrant population, their U.S.-born children, or accessed via fraud. The study tallies the impact on education, medical, justice/enforcement, welfare and other government programs. The report notes that the $116 billion cost of illegal immigration

---

* https://fairus.org/issue/publications-resources/fiscal-burden-illegal-immigration-united-states-taxpayers. (September 27, 2017, Washington, D.C.)

falls on state and local taxpayers disproportionately – by a ratio of roughly 2 to 1 – with state and local expenditures totaling $88.9 billion and Federal expenditures totaling $45.8 billion, with only approximately $19 billion recouped in taxes. Need I say more.

The Taxes Paid by Illegal Immigrant Workers Don't Cover the Costs

The report also tallies the taxes paid by the 7 million illegal immigrants in the workforce, estimating that 35 percent of them are operating in the underground economy and noting that these workers have no payroll taxes deducted from their earnings.

The study finds that taxes paid by illegal immigrants are five times as likely to wind up in federal coffers than in state and local treasuries. Total taxes paid to the federal government by illegal immigrants totaled $15.4 billion, with state and local governments receiving approximately $3.5 billion, even though these entities bear a disproportionate share of the burden.

Other Key Findings:

- The staggering total costs of illegal immigrants and their children outweigh the taxes paid to federal and state governments by a ratio of roughly 7 to 1, with costs at nearly $135 billion compared to tax revenues at nearly $19 billion.
- All told, the nearly $135 billion paid out by federal and state and local taxpayers to cover the cost of the presence of 12.5 million illegal aliens and their 4.2 million citizen children amounts to approximately $8,075 per illegal alien and citizen child prior to taxes paid, or $6,940 per person after taxes are paid.
- On the federal level, medical ($17.14 billion) is by far the highest cost, with law enforcement coming second ($13.15 billion) and general government services ($8 billion) third.
- At the state and local level, education ($44.4 billion) was by far the largest expense, followed by general public services ($18.5 billion) and medical ($12.1 billion).
- The study also includes cost and tax revenue estimates

per state. The top three states based on total cost to state taxpayers for illegal immigrants and their children: California ($23 billion); Texas ($10.9 billion), and New York ($7.5 billion).

Illegals And Crime

There has been much rhetoric from the left and the open-borders lobby pushing for more illegal immigration to suggest that illegal immigrants pose no threat to the safety and security of this nation and commit fewer crimes than their legal immigrant counterparts and US citizens.

If one watches the network newscasts, the ideologues and open-borders surrogates consistently accuse Americans and law enforcement experts who suggest otherwise of being racist, anti-immigration xenophobes. If you pay attention to the rhetoric, you will find one item glaringly missing — facts.

Research conducted by the federal government oversight organization Judicial Watch in 2014 documented that 50 percent of all federal crimes were committed near our border with Mexico. Of the 61,529 criminal cases filed by federal prosecutors; 40 percent or 24,746 were in court districts along the southern borders of California, Arizona and Texas.

The U.S. Department of Justice documents that in 2014, 19 percent or over 12,000 criminal cases filed by prosecutors were for violent crimes; and over 22 percent or 13,300 cases were for drug related felonies. That same year, the U.S. Sentencing Commission found that 75 percent of all criminal defendants who were convicted and sentenced for federal drug offenses were illegal immigrants. Illegal immigrants were also involved in 17 percent of all drug trafficking sentences and one third of all federal prison sentences.

The U.S. Department of Justice and the U.S. Sentencing Commission reported that as of 2014, illegal immigrants were convicted and sentenced for over 13 percent of all crimes committed in the U.S. According to the FBI, 67,642 murders were committed in the U.S. from 2005 through 2008, and 115,717 from 2003 through 2009. The General Accounting Office documents that criminal immigrants committed 25,064 of these murders.

To extrapolate from these statistics, this means that just over 3.5 percent of the population unlawfully residing in the U.S. committed 22 percent to 37 percent of all murders in the nation. This is astounding.

In California alone, over 2,400 illegal immigrants out of a total prison population of 130,000 are in the state's prison system for the crime of homicide.

Recent crime analysis by both the Department of Homeland Security (DHS) and Texas law enforcement authorities indicate that between June 2011 and March 2017, over 217,000 criminal immigrants were arrested and booked into Texas jails.

In researching the criminal careers of these defendants, it was revealed that they had jointly committed over nearly 600,000 criminal offenses. Their arrests included nearly 1,200 homicides; almost 69,000 assaults; 16,854 burglaries; 700 kidnappings; nearly 6,200 sexual assaults; 69,000 drug offenses; 8,700 weapons violations; over 3,800 robberies and over 45,000 obstructing police charges. In determining the status of these offenders in the U.S., it was confirmed by DHS that over 173,000 or 66 percent of these immigrant criminal defendants were in our country illegally at the times of their arrests.

According to research and statistics by the U.S. Departments of Justice and Homeland Security, U.S. taxpayers are footing an annual bill of nearly $19 million a day to house and care for an estimated 300,000 to 450,000 convicted criminal immigrants who are eligible for deportation and are currently residing in local jails and state and federal prisons across the country.

So the next time you hear some Open Borders politician or pro illegal immigrant surrogates advocate on their behalf, ask yourself why we as American citizens need to bear the increasing costs of violence, victimization and burdensome taxes in subsidizing illegal immigrant criminals who shouldn't be in our country in the first place.* (Reference – Ron Martinelli)

"Illegal aliens who commit additional crimes in the United States are a threat to public safety and a burden on our criminal justice system," said Attorney General Jeff Sessions. "This is

---

* The truth about illegal aliens and crime in America, Ron Martinelli, Ph.D. https://drronmartinelli.com/2017/04/10/the-truth-about-illegal-aliens-and-crime-in-the-u-s/

why we must secure our borders with walls and effective law enforcement. We must strengthen cooperation between federal, state and local governments as we strive to fulfill our sacred duty of protecting and serving the American people." Additionally our sovereignty suffers.

Sanctuary Cities

There is no clear definition of a "sanctuary city" and there is no clear understanding of how our immigration laws got to be so contradictory. It is not illegal to be an "undocumented immigrant," but what, then, is an "illegal immigrant"? A "sanctuary city" is generally one where the local officials do not fully cooperate with federal officials who are responsible for controlling immigration; instead, they seek to protect immigrants from being deported. This is difficult to comprehend and certainly in opposition to the American way.

Yet there are mayors who erroneously defend this principle as though it threatens their personal freedom or perhaps their ability to obtain votes. It is difficult to comprehend the ignorance of the judiciary. Liberal judges are in favor of the sanctuary city. The situation of sanctuary city is a state of insanity. Dangerous criminals walk the streets when honest citizens are at risk. Beyond any shadow of doubt this condition is just one additional characteristic of The Massaging of Reality.

Surprise! Sanctuary cities do, indeed, experience higher crime rates than do non-sanctuary cities, an in-depth WND has developed this data of the most recent study of the question reveals. An August 2016 study of the relationship between "sanctuary city" policies and crime rates shows that cities refusing to cooperate with federal immigration authorities consistently have significantly higher violent crimes rates than do non-sanctuary cities with similar populations and demographics, WND has found.

The study, published last fall by researchers from the University of California-Riverside and Highline College in Des Moines, Washington, is frequently cited by proponents of "sanctuary cities" who ignore or downplay one important detail – the actual crime statistics of the carefully selected cities chosen for the comparison model.

An analysis of the data by WND reveals that non-sanctuary cities comparable in population, size and demographics consistently – year over year – experience and report lower percentages of violent crime as well as lower percentages of property crimes.

Violent crime rates are, in fact, drastically higher in sanctuary cities than their non-sanctuary counterparts, as is evidenced by the chart the authors used to delineate their conclusion.

The violent crime rate in sanctuary cities, as indicated above, dramatically increased after sanctuary city policy was enacted, and even doubled in some cases. The researchers found "similar results for property crime property crime and rape."

According to the Department of Homeland Security, from January 2014 to August 2014, more than 8,145 aliens were released from jail after arrest after their respective jurisdictions declined an immigration detainer request from Immigration and Customs Enforcement. Sixty-two percent of them had a prior criminal record, and 3,000 of them were felons. Of the 8,145 individuals released, 1,867 were subsequently re-arrested a total of 4,298 times and accumulated a staggering 7,491 charges. (Source: The Politics of Refuge: Sanctuary Cities, Crime and Undocumented Immigration; Aug.16, 2016. Data based on FBI crime statistics)

Thus the remaining chapters are even more important, as they teach the principle of utilizing self-awareness which is necessary for the individual to COPE with a problematic culture. All that is recorded is material under which I have been trained and have researched during my entire period of adulthood with my PhD in Management and Psychology. I am anxious to share all of my knowledge and experience to Americans to make the best of their rightful opportunity. Mr. Trump will take care of the rest.

Chapter 4. The Challenge Of A Problematic Culture

We are now ready to take a further concentrated view of the issue of the elusive contemporary culture. Of course there is more to it than accepting the supposition that it makes sense to give illegal immigrants a driver's license and other rights, and the inclination to leave our hair ungroomed and leave our shirts untucked and unbuttoned.

Having identified some of the facets of The Facial Hair and Cleavage Culture, we will take a look at how to cope with all the negative input from our surroundings. Fundamentally, if you are aware how to remove this threat by coping, you will possess a very positive delivery status to the pros and cons of the major cause of the cultural problem. The latter mode leads to peace and happiness.

Our culture is being swept along by a rapid, out of control, and not necessarily friendly set of trends. It is constantly in an excessive state of negative change. Many individuals are not aware of its complexity and its magnitude. Large segments of the US-born population increasingly feel they're living in a foreign, confusing, unpleasant country, and that includes while they are surrounded by people of their own kind, within their own ethnic group, if they can find such an enclave.

In fact I am quite unhappy with the present state. If I stop to really pay attention to my feelings, I find myself in discomfort bordering on a state of tension. I constantly make an effort to improve my method of coping, always keeping in mind the aim of finding a comfortable solution. I am constantly aware of the new environment and always searching for the proper codes of coping. I refuse to be negative in spite of the fact that the current cultural environment is rejected by me and does not fit in my world. So I must divest the negative side and move on. After consideration and control, I am convinced that I have attained the correct profile to avoid relative tension.

Open criticism to my associates is totally unacceptable. Most people are determined to take the easiest path, they'd rather struggle to "move with the flow" than take the trouble to figure out what they believe is good and right, and stand up for that. No, to point out the flaws of the society around us would lead them to label me as a deficient human being.

Consequently I have become somewhat of a controlled introvert and I publicly avoid the subject in total in order to be socially acceptable. However, it pains me to see how unaware young people are of what is going on. Yet the problem is not accepted as a topic for conversation, perhaps in part because people are afraid. When any difference of views pops up, we no longer have the skills and confidence to calmly talk the issue through. People feel threatened or feel like they're being accused of something, rather than being open to explore a different perspective.

Plus, the issues I have in mind are totally unrecognized by the majority. Since I want to enjoy life until the age of 100, I am consistent in avoiding commentary to my younger associates regarding my opinion of the negative, out of control culture which is in a complete state of no recognition.

What have I learned from my peaceful advantaged state of wisdom? First of all the younger groups don't recognize how society is being weakened, how Americans are being kept in a state of adolescence, and how the negative eruptions of the culture weigh upon everybody, contributing to tension, anxiety, insecurity and depression. Of course, these negative states of mind are completely debilitating, making it more difficult to find a job, form a family, and organize one's life for success and fulfillment.

In my opinion, the issue is seriously out of control. So I stand without comment and try to take an attitude that states "Let the culture flow." Most important I am trained to decipher Reality and continue the path to peace and happiness for myself and my family.

It is my responsibility however to provide my reader how to cope within the complete voyage of Reality, and offer some wisdom on how to achieve the objective of happiness without conflict. You might say I am a spy embedded in the USA's problematic culture movement. Actually, I am undercover. This enables me to maintain an advantageous vantage point from which I can practice my elder wisdom. I must not become lost in the confusion and the complexity of this culture but help others to avoid unwelcome tension. So follow carefully with my message.

A key point for me is to acknowledge that I cannot change or control the movement. I stand by and let it roll. I am out of the game. Life can be undesirable in many ways, particularly for the senior citizen. So I live intellectually in a safety zone of comprehension.

However the first step in coping is to understand the existence of this culture, its characteristics, and the ramifications

Protecting Yourself

These are the steps for getting into the habit of being aware and positive.

1. Wake up, pay attention and think about what's going on. Be aware and comprehend.

2. Maintain awareness and understanding.

3. Avoid complaining; nobody wants to hear it.

4. Stay away from public demonstrations. They often end in violence.

5. Maintain a constant state of overall recognition and improvement.

6. Smile, be friendly and do not create a controversy.

The primary purpose of these cautionary notes is to offer a peaceful alternative based on consideration for others and avoid creating tension and conflict. In time, once you've established a degree of comfort with another person, you might test the waters by carefully introducing a discussion regarding the New Culture. At this point you possess fundamental comprehension and judgment of when and how to open up a discussion.

The above is the smart list of behaviors for the outsider. Stay on the sidelines of the non-constructive aspects of our fast-changing culture. Be content with your ability to arrive at your own understanding of what it is.

That may sound like a surrender. In actuality it is a positive and healthy way of coping with a monstrous perpetual and undesirable condition. Live by the truism of the guaranteed magnitude of our teachings. It's most important to understand that this movement is in a critical, sensitive state. The latter is a constant Reality and where it will end up is impossible to predict. The best I can do is to provide definition as a part of one's awareness which is the profile necessary for the elimination of stress. The recommended list above provides the prescription for eventual coping and is the best alternative. Follow a peaceful positive role that breaks down the will of the ignorant. Also this approach leads to an opportunity to lead others. Avoid offering assistance too early, to avoid rejection.

Conducting ourselves as peaceful and positive role models, we offer a profile for the young to follow. The goal must be the delivery of a culture of positive values.

In this chapter I'll add to the sketch of our definition of the existing American culture. Then you'll be prepared to augment this review with your introductory information regarding coping. So consequently as we move through this chapter on the culture I suggest that you take the advantage of applying some of the coping techniques already discussed.

Having identified the basic elements previously, our next objective is to provide a clear definition of where the state of our culture is at the present time. However I will now constantly touch on the subject of coping. I will further offer interesting commentary is based on my constant observations. Facial hair on men and revealing décolleté necklines for women seem to me to be expressions of insecurity, in fact, and they are signs that the individuals involved wish to join a group for comfort and security.

There are no particular reasons for this selection, and the supposition that such choices will somehow offer a sense of belonging is erroneous. Careful grooming shows self-respect and calls forth respect from others. Yet the practice of negligence, or the appearance of being negligent, is widespread and fostered by the negative environment.

The same holds true for the insouciant style of leaving one's shirt untucked. These new cultural behaviors contribute nothing to the intellectual endeavor but possibly are believed to offer a sense of togetherness and safety, to some degree, in shark infested waters.

Focus On Your Own Attitude

My primary purpose in this chapter is not to be a purveyor of unhappiness from a disgusting Reality. However, I do comprehend the critical status of our culture and how it affects the citizen. While there were abuses of various kinds, by comparison, the past society was pristine. With the current population the issue of perfection does not begin to be a consideration.

It is important to recognize that our philosophy of America is freedom and the right to the pursuit of happiness. Our founding fathers were very serious in the meaning of the latter. Needless to say, many of them gave their lives for these values. For the people and by the people was a serious adage, but it has become scarce in application. So therefore it has been my objective in this chapter to develop a case history in order to teach the citizens who are now in a strange country to learn how to cope and to enjoy longevity. If I am found guilty of anything, then I accept that status. What I find more important is that I am a true patriot, sincerely looking to help my fellow countrymen.

I don't believe that in the current environment I have the wherewithal to enjoy the pursuit of happiness. That is now unattainable. At the same time I have introduced a behavioral pattern that is not detrimental and permits the citizen to cope, on a daily, successful basis. We have to avoid internal stress and discomfort, which are a total negative and contrary to peace, happiness and longevity.

The task of demonstrating the uncertainty and the effect of the present day culture has been clearly defined.

Life In Post-War America

After the Armistice I returned to the USA in 1947 at the age of 25. Approximately 60 million people of various countries were killed in World War II, 20 million military and civilian deaths in the USSR alone. Yugoslavia lost 1 million, military and civilians. And the US lost over 418,000 fighting men. Upon my return at the time, and considering where I'd been, I must say that America really struck me as beautiful. The society was tight-knit and positive through out. There was a sincere rush to get back to normal; and since we gained more than we lost in this war, that was relatively easy. People quickly put the war in the past and most families keenly looked ahead and responded in that manner.

However, I had volunteered in the US Navy and served in the Atlantic and the Pacific Campaigns. Those of us who had actually been engaged in the fighting did face difficulties. When I arrived home, I could not sleep or be without stress. I had to divest the military profile. So therefore I departed home and converted my life to that of a hobo. This change seemed to work very well for me and gave me the opportunity to find myself as a civilian.

I slept in hobo jungles, washed myself at gas station restrooms and traveled the USA, throughout New England and Eastern Canada. I slept on porches of abandoned homes or in "hobo jungles." When in the latter, before retiring at night I would pull out my long knife and stick it in the ground near my head in preparedness.

Six months later I was totally altered and was ready to become a civilian. I had witnessed the USA from a lonely, variable, and lowly vantage point which reminded me how much my family and home meant to me as a place of peace and tranquility. The hobo culture is a physically demanding one where unidentified murders occur every day. I must admit there were two attempts on myself, which I did not allow.

From all of my experiences at that point, I could attest to

a powerful culture of togetherness that prevailed in America which waited for me to join. My taking time off to travel had served me well and I was back to normal. Courtesy, decency, concern for others prevailed in the home atmosphere. I will never forget the USA at that time as a country of togetherness, united by the joint effort and the shared sacrifices resulting from the war, and united by the sense of relief that it was over, and we'd won.

The difference between 1947 and today is beyond comprehension and a sad observation. There doesn't seem to be any motivation today to move back to that culture. The movement of Facial Hair and Cleavage Culture is the predominant, significant one available and it is growing. Unfortunately it is not recognized as a negative culture and receives very little comments regarding the pros and cons.

Here is a short list of healthy values, in no particular order. 1. Family. 2. Health. 3. God. 4. Reality. 5. Patriotism. 6. Self-Esteem. 7. Concern For Others. 8. Charity.

Chapter 5. The Beacons Of Wisdom

At this juncture I will comment on the nature of the different attitudes between the young and the old. I have labeled these elements as the Beacons of Wisdom, primarily since there is difference in how the beacons of wisdom are in process.

The Beginning And The End

One important philosophy regarding life is what I call "The Beginning and The End" to everything in the universe. This viewpoint applies to all facets of life. Unfortunately there is a beginning and end to everything, and for the most part, people really come to grips with this fact far too late. It happens fast. For example you buy a brand new car, and overnight it has become "pre-owned." It doesn't take that much time before the nomenclature "clunker" is appropriate. And finally, the real end approaches and your "new" car is feed for the cruncher.

How about marriage and partnership? Look back over a span of years and look ahead to how much time you hope is left. Life slips by in an instant! When the Day of Parting arrives for a loving couple, a complication arises. There is a survivor who no longer has a partner.

If the marriage was positive, and especially if it was long lasting, then the survivor beyond question has personal obstacles to overcome. (On average, people are getting married later and later in life; yet some still manage to stay together for 40 or 50 years, and they did not get used to the dreary experience of solitary existence as young adults.) One of the primary difficulties is loneliness. The only way to assuage that is by making it a priority to fill your days with a fulfilling activity.

What To Live For?

This leads to a critical question, "Do I have something to live for?" Each one of us needs to prepare in advance for the simple and obvious fact that we may be the one stuck in this situation. The survivor needs to have imagined and thought through various scenarios and plans beforehand, in order to be able to go on to a new fulfilling life in a positive manner.

In addition to the stress of the process of grieving and the burden of bureaucratic details that come with the death of a spouse or partner, there is also the burden of the New Culture. The shock of finding oneself in the new role of a single person is not eased by the negative environment which in itself immerses us in an unpleasant, debilitating condition.

Having "something to live for" is essential, and we must find or invent that something for ourselves. That is a fundamental element of coping, so this chapter is elevated to this special situation where the Day of Partition is a preoccupation while the Empire is in a state of decline. This double burden must be overcome for all parties.

In my case I had 67 years of happy marriage, which cannot be reconstructed in a relationship with a newer acquaintance. Thus I became a survivor in the single state. Here was my plan. I will continue my personal life in balance, as in the past, which centered around organic food, proper exercise and a positive attitude. My experiences are such that I continue to have wonderful remembrances of my marriage and I overwhelmingly miss my partner.

So in this new singular lifestyle, what must I do in order to cope? I made a plan when my Lady became ill from a stroke; she passed on eight years thereafter. I took care of her for eight years. It was during that period that I began to think under the banner, "What do I have to live for?" Number one on the list is to be sure that you are truly in accord with yourself and have something planned to live for, coping adequately for any additional challenges.

In my youth, I studied music and played in the big bands of the 40s. Later I attended night school and achieved a PhD in management and psychology. From this short sketch I concluded that I would compose music, write books and create poetry, and thus have something to live for. And indeed, by now I have been published in all these categories, with nine books already out. I plan to continue this activity for the rest of my visit on earth.

My writing mostly centered around research in corporate row for 43 years, along with my studies in music ‑ at one time I thought I would devote my total career to music. The war changed that. I believe first and foremost before we can discuss numerable categories of longevity, it is necessary to have planned in advance the proposition titled "Having something to live for."

The loneliness and the change of lifestyle are critical mental impediments to overcome. Therefore number one on the opening list is to be sure that you are fully in accord and aware for the need to have something to live for. Having experienced the all‑encompassing phenomenon of this change,

I can honestly say that without books, music and poetry, I would not have reached my current status. This complication was beyond anything that I have experienced in 95 years. Of course there will be features beyond these chapters to fully explain the multifaceted techniques of winning with full comprehension of coping with the New Culture. At this moment values are receiving top consideration.

Being Alone

Solitude is the most difficult portion of this experience. No matter how many friends or relatives you have, there will be quiet moments in your life when the past and its wonderful memories overcome your thoughts. It is impossible to eliminate this situation even though I am busy in my work. In order to illustrate what I mean, allow me the opportunity to specifically outline the Playing Field by recreating my experiences since the

Day of parting in some detail.

In order to support my statement regarding solitude and having something to live for, I present an exacting review which is offered as part of the total presentation of important material for my reader. Many examples of the past will be used as part of the material to continue the issue of "what do I have to live for" which is included in the element of Coping.

Challenges After The Day Of Parting

We now continue with the analysis of the Beacons of Wisdom per se. We use the word Beacon because we teach to lighten the burden of the various phases in life. One might describe the Beacons of Wisdom as follows. It is important to understand the various phases of the required lifestyle. The word beacon suggests a light designating the path to knowledge and understanding of Reality.

There is a lot of Reality that we do not face until the day of parting occurs. For example, under the conditions of The New Culture, some matters require full application of the art of coping, and you have to know how to cope before the need arises. So therefore I bring this matter to the cognizance of the reader that under this condition it is critically important to move forward with the techniques of coping. Once you are overwhelmed by negative circumstances, it will be far more difficult to learn new ways to behave and new ways frames of reference through which to view events. By preparing in advance, you step beyond the hardships of the New Culture.

However while coping with the complete challenge of the New Culture, we cannot overlook other responsibilities. To further explain coping following the day of parting, here are a few of the key challenges.

1. Society. As a duo, you had a certain number of friends. Unfortunately duos are not compatible with singles. The majority of your friends who are duos will disappear since their motives and objectives are in a social category that does not work well with singles. Consequently I can count on one hand the number of "loyals" that have remained as part of my societal group. Singles cannot very well run with the pack of duos.

2. Property. You've owned a house and land for many years. The interior is filled with memories and the only conclusion is to both sell the physical goods and lose most of the reminders of your "real life." In selling a house, psychologically you feel that the experience is an invasion of your privacy. I never believed that I would become so attached to my home, but it was too large for one inhabitant. When people came to inspect the property, I felt resentment and an invasion of my privacy. Nevertheless, where there is no choice, you must adjust.

3. Contents. Here, I refer to antiques and vintage furniture, table items, artwork, and so forth. If you have real valuables, some of them would be worth having appraised before selling, in order to have a reasonable idea of their value. Of course, another shock will come if you find that your "priceless" collection is of little value to today's households. Truthfully, many of our "treasures" are now available on eBay and other Internet sites where one quickly learns they cannot be sold for anything approaching what we think their value is. The new generations cannot afford antique furniture that requires care and maintenance; and they expect to have to move more often than the older generations have done.

I hired a team that was accustomed to selling such things and they had a resume beyond expectation. But their goal was to clear the house for the realtors, rather than to get me top dollar.. Consequently they measure their success by their ability to clear the house prior to the realtors' entry. They set "giveaway" prices to clear the property. It's true that the house has to be cleared, one way or another, but seeing your treasured possessions gathered up by strangers is an appalling experience.

4. The Property Sale. There is one particularly unpleasant aspect to the selling of the property that often comes as a tremendous and dismaying surprise. Many states require a home inspection before the sale is completed. A special inspector comes and develops a long list for "repair and replace." Not only is this a shock but it obviously can cost the seller a substantial amount of funds to meet the requirements. The house cannot be sold until the seller takes care of the all of the items on the list. The sale is held up, throwing a monkey wrench into everyone's plans, from cash flow to scheduling the move-out and move-in.

5. Nostalgia. Your home was filled with furniture, pictures, collections, finery, garments and other items that you are not going to be able to keep with you, from specific souvenirs to simple everyday items that are precious because they are so familiar to you. When the house and property is finally sold, you drive by your old home every now and then to fulfill your nostalgia.

6. Apartment. When the house is sold, you need a dwelling, so you travel the apartment circuit and find that you must pay a shocking amount monthly for just the basics. It will be necessary to be prepared for a completely different lifestyle due to limited space and convenience.

7. Doctors. As time goes by, it is Reality and expectation that health begins to break down somewhat. Maladies that you acquired in your former life may become a problem. An example is heart disease. There is an old saying that having heart disease is no guarantee for tomorrow. Longevity depends greatly on your state of health. Hence the necessity to follow the rules during your early years as well as later. I see an internist every three to six months.

8. Food. Most likely you will now be the purchaser and the chef, even if you were not before. It is absolutely necessary to become proficient in this task. A useful way to think of this is to become your own chef and restaurant in the apartment, although I must say that the latter is "No fun."

9. Clothes. When I moved to my apartment, I carefully brought with me several suits and the accoutrements that go with them. In one year I have dressed up just one time, and I have been invited out less than six times. A single man cannot run with the pack.

Thus we close our comments on Coping for the elderly. Your life changes and there is a definite alteration in your overall profile. At this point it is critical to adjust. Comparing the past to the present is nothing more than a recognition of Reality, whereby life's alterations are recognized and we move on.

The question of longevity arises and how will this be affected. I can say from my own experience that the righteous coping way brings happiness, steadfastness and reduces stress. In addition I can take a step further and say that Negativisms and Conflict are far from the wisdom choice. The danger is that the negative condition is here to stay and is growing. There are no automatic actions or solutions that seem to reverse this problem according to the growing level of negative action. I have stated earlier that I have demonstrated my bio at the beginning of chapter 1. In order to provide evidence that in spite of all the negatives the individual can find righteousness by refusing to compromise your self-respect while achieving the American Dream.

The major problem is that what I have just described provides evidence that the masses fail to think in the terms of the Three Fabulous Synonyms. Lies have overtaken truth, self-worth is out of consideration. Honesty is by no means a serious consideration. No matter where you turn in our current culture all the above is in action while there is limited self-awareness by the individual. In the long term this damaging factor if not resolved will multiply itself further and America First will be in a state of the impossible. Our current leadership by taking corrective steps may reverse the trend. It is our only hope and certainly with all this tension longevity will suffer. We need honest Leadership. Mr. Trump is our only Hope.

In closing this chapter it is important to summarize this material in an effective consolidated fashion which will aid in further comprehension:

1. Self-esteem is compromised daily and is beyond awareness. A malady that self-control, internal thought and awareness would be a state of consciousness and a tremendous aid to finding reality.

2. We are obliged to make yes/no decisions at every turn, and this is part of a natural long term challenge. The following is a small diagrammatic solution of this facet.

3. A concern for self-worth will decisively advise you which conclusion is correct and of proper behavior and philosophy, so you know how to select the correct value.

4. The pause to consider self-esteem is, in the end, the savior of the individual. Unfortunately people today have forgotten and/or lacks the courage to take a good hard look the choices they make.

5. If you follow the above, your psyche is at peace, tranquil, guaranteeing a happy life of longevity. Where do you stand?

6. In this recommended process, pressure is eliminated. Guilt is nonexistent and self-esteem is not compromised. You are on the way to the American Dream.

Over the past several years I have lectured throughout the world. My major commentary centers around the human capacity of inner concentration and self-awareness. The latter is a necessary state of maintaining health in recognition of the emphasis of the Three Fabulous Synonyms and the achievement of peace and tranquility. With emphasis it is important again to caution that there are several additional important parts of the above process which awaits you as follows.

Self-awareness is a trait and the basis for the good life and can be utilized in unlimited quantity. My favorite saying is "If you don't see it or hear it, it never happened." Seeing and hearing are the components of self-awareness following full consideration and analysis of the incoming data.

The human being has five senses: 1. seeing, 2. hearing, 3. touch, 4. taste and 5. smell. Items one and two are the most critical to self-awareness.

There is a sixth, called common sense. Even though it's an unofficial sense, it should never be omitted from any matter. Common sense is an extremely important extension of self-awareness. Dealing with the Three Fabulous Synonyms requires constant self-awareness in all facets of the proposition at hand and must never be side stepped.

The basic concept lies in Robinson's Law, which is, "Think Up Front and Live Easy." Simply said if you are fully aware your life will be with minimum tension. An additional aspect of self-awareness includes a clear vision of Reality which is the way things really are. In facing a situation you must call upon your Reality for assistance. Clarity is a critical element of this process to be sure that there is no personal Bias that provides an erroneous state. This element simplifies a great number of life's problems. If you possess a highly developed vision of Reality and behave accordingly, there will be less tension in your life which is a boon to peace and happiness.

The person with this firm understanding and behavior pattern should certainly move successfully through challenges.

As the elder in my family (of course I have grandchildren and other relatives), I am the source of the Beacons of Wisdom, which I am happy to make available and teach. My status as the family elder is without tension and filled with personal satisfaction and respect. Probably the most critical element in this treatise thus far is the need for the individual to consistently refuse to compromise the Three Synonyms. The Critical Three always relieve tension, providing comfort and aiding in personal relaxation. Therefore 95 Years Young becomes a realistic goal that is promoted throughout this text. It is my hope that the reader will find revelations and expanded knowledge in an area that is commonly over looked.

Needless to say in our current culture there are many typical situations that are, unfortunately, not even recognized. This treatise is your opportunity to become Aware and involved in the use of many elements of life that are critical to long term happiness and tranquility. Never subordinate the Beacon of Wisdom. It is never too late to begin. In closing, the Lefties' philosophy is penetrating our daily events while the New Culture takes advantage of the situation by invading with strength while receiving assistance in training. The Beacons of Wisdom are clearly a critical element to facilitate coping.

CHAPTER 6. THE CODES OF BEHAVIOR MANIFESTO

By "codes of behavior" I mean human values, and I'll use both terms interchangeably. Now, let's consider the word manifesto. This chapter discusses a factor of life that is by no means a suggestion or recommendation. It is a mandatory requirement which is built in to every individual in the universe. There is no avoidance or compromise to this manifesto. You operate according to your values, whether you know it or not.

Unfortunately, most of the time, most of us don't consciously think about our values and they become an automatic part of our decision-making — or are allowed to wither — without our exercising judgment and responsibility. So therefore regarding the future, it is difficult to predict most outcomes. For success in this universe, this unseen manifesto clearly requires the individual must, for a lifetime, adopt certain values for the better. Much of your set of values will accrue automatically without prior consideration. Unfortunately, this is the best we have. We as humans need to make a conscious effort to develop awareness of our existing Codes of Behavior and to change them when we see they are inadequate. Furthermore, fulfilling the Manifesto is equally critical.

Code Of Behavior Manifesto

"I hereby promise myself to adopt only positive and healthy values. I will take inventory frequently and consciously as I participate in their utilization, making improvements as often as possible. I must through awareness modify my values inventory to assure that those around me are benefited along with myself." End of Manifesto. The correct fundamental is to acquire a value set that is satisfactory to yourself and influences your behavior, and consequently becoming a matter of sharing your values with others.

When babies are born they are primarily in a three- mode existence: Eat, Sleep and Love. With the passing of time the child commences to demonstrate a few Codes of Behavior. This short list for the most part remains within the family and is not contested. Yet the development is in process for that of a potential adult. At this age the parent is the coach, teaching modification to the value set with love. The adoption of codes during this early state is simplified in application until in young maturity the child interacts with others automatically while accepting and rejecting Codes Of Behavior. This process expands with time and by full maturity is well into application with a variety of results forming a personality. The process can be heavily influenced with guidance.

Unfortunately, this continuous process of adopting of Codes of Behavior in a modification/rejection process often goes on automatically, without Awareness. It is at this point in its early stage and continuing throughout the future that the execution of the Manifesto of the Codes of Behavior takes place forever. Even at age 95, whenever I become aware that a modification is due, I happily respond in a positive mode of acceptance.

The young adult (and beyond) is exposed to a multitude of value situations that can be accepted or rejected. Through awareness and experience, the mature individual will continue to adjust the value set. However the stubborn human - and there are such people - will stay with a current inventory, with inner objection to any modification.

To enjoy a tranquil life, the person must develop a Codes of Behavior Inventory that minimizes Tension. It is important in order to constantly fulfill the Manifesto. The individual must constantly be aware of the effectiveness in a multitude of situations. Later in this chapter we outline a number of types of individuals that assuredly demonstrate several separate predispositions to a Code of Behavior Inventory. Unfortunately, this is evidence of serious difficulties in our culture.

Further it is critical to remember that there are positive and negative values. Just look at the people you admire, or whose company you enjoy, and think about how you would characterize how they think, talk, and how they conduct themselves. Then think about some of the people you know whose presence does not give you a boost. What would you say about how they think, talk and behave? Draw up some lists, and keep them at hand. You can always ponder where you fit in, and keep on working to improve yourself.

In everyday life it is common practice for an individual to interact with all kinds of individuals, professionals, non professionals, managers, non managers and rank and file individuals. Needless to say, a great number of values are acceptable to all types of people and yet are not necessarily Common Codes. So the fundamental principle comes forward that, first of all, you must adopt only favorable primary values.

There is a litany of values that are common and acceptable to all. Values acceptable to people in all walks of life include the following:

> Security
> Opportunity
> Leadership
> Comfort
> Persuasive
> Happiness
> Love of family
> Courteous
> Dignity
> Togetherness
> Forgiving
> Cooperation
> Fairness
> Safety
> Friendship
> Respect
> Sincerity
> Communication

Trust

In general, everyone feels good with a person who is:

Positive

Courageous

Informative

Enthusiastic

In spite of differences between people's standing in society, for the most part all positive Codes of Behavior are acceptable to everyone. An important dynamic to recognize is that no matter of differences in your manner of living and social status for the most part all positive Codes of Behavior are interchangeable and acceptable to all parties.

In the following list we show some of the values that are considered positive and are accepted throughout Western society, among daily workers, management, professionals, retirees, government, and people associating for non-work-related activities. All these people hold in common a set of exceptionally important Codes of Behavior. Values like Kindness, Respect and Friendliness are acceptable to all, and when interacting with others, of course, it helps to utilize these values. There are many positive interactions that are brought forth by utilizing the Common Codes of Behavior.

If you wish to be Welcome and Right, this information is the solution. A manager of a business would be the favorite if that individual utilizes Common Codes frequently. The problem arises when the person behaves according to codes that are outside of human acceptance. Allow me to illustrate how it works, using a few case histories that demonstrate critical positive results by utilization of accepted Common Codes.

Case History 1

As the leader of a manufacturing operation, I interacted with all members of the enterprise. One day we had an accident in which an employee was moving a pallet of finished product. This load was overturned and the entire load of finished product was destroyed, a value of $7,000. I ordered the trucker to be fired, particularly when a friend advised me that the trucker was using narcotics and could very well cause another accident.

The union pointed out that discharging him was excessive and not warranted. We conducted three grievance meetings and the next step would require we go to Arbitration. My experience with this government association was inadequate; I didn't expect the arbiters to be so superficial, making decisions without proper understanding of the special nature of our environment. I dived into my experience to see how I could best respond. Lo and behold, Common Codes of Behavior would to be my final response. I stated as follows - to a belligerent group: The act in question destroyed $7,000 worth of product and caused a threat your safety and mine. Such accidents are certainly rare, so it is difficult to accept that it was unavoidable. The importance of your security and mine is the issue in this case, and my decision to discharge was taken in that vein. The union agreed. The union boss came over and shook my hand and walked out of the meeting, never to interfere in the matter again.

Case History 2

Here is an important case history whereby a testy situation was settled by virtue of bringing to the attention of both parties the essence of the Common Codes of Behavior. This is an example whereby calling on the Common Codes raised to the consciousness of both union and the management the fact that important values were at stake that were critical to both parties.

One day I came to work and found that we had a traffic problem, caused by the fact that the workers were marching up and down the sidewalk. There was a strike, related to a matter pertaining to the industrial relations area, who were responsible for managing the negotiations. As I stood on the steps of the plant, I obviously looked very upset. The leader of the strike came over to me with the following message. He said, "I see you are upset, so just say the word and I will call the strike off for you." I concentrated for a few minutes and I made the following reply. "You folks are fighting for something you believe in. I do not have the right to accept your gracious offer and destroy a value that's important to the rank and file. I appreciate your friendship and your consideration, but I cannot accept your offer with due conscience." We shook hands and he departed. The strike was eventually settled and all was normal again.

In considering the well-meant offer, I resorted to the issue of Common Codes. Here was the matter in codes that was diametrically opposing. The strike was an acceptable strategy, of value to the union but not to me. And even though a sincere offer was made, I was highly influenced by the fact that I didn't have the moral right to be selfish and overlook this Code of Behavior that was part of the union inventory. Once again, consideration of the other person was my value system, which I could not set aside; and I behaved in that manner which overtly expressed to my rank and file friends that I value their needs equal to mine.

My next objective is to prepare a value scale to demonstrate with emphasis three levels of the utilization of values.

The Value Scale

GOOD – self-esteem, honest, friendly, caring, courteous, communicative.

BAD – no self-esteem, dishonest, shady, non-communicative, untruthful.

UGLY – low energy, overweight, no self-esteem, untrusting, prone to drink or smoke (I include here marijuana), nervous and with a low level of self-awareness.

The three categories good, bad and ugly are by no means atypical. You can be in the presence of any one of the three and become aware very quickly of where the other person stands. Unfortunately, this variance of conditions is surprisingly frequent in our society and can cover the majority of categories of value sets. Is it likely that you will take these latter individuals aside and attempt to make them aware of their problem? The chances of having a receptive listener are definitely low.

However, if you have concentrated on the descriptions and the differences, the result is that you are now properly equipped. With this recognition you should gain strength from any of these vantage points. The good is to be congratulated and strengthened. The other two categories, for sure you are now aware and in a position to reject them. This diagram encourages righteous behavior from all points of view and helps promote the ability to achieve peace and tranquility. It is a perpetual source of wisdom. I aim to place this idea in as many frames as possible during this entire treatise. Daily life as time passes throughout the years should be with happiness, self-esteem, security, love and on and on.

Self-awareness and the activity of Common Codes are key pillars of the successful life. The average person does not think about things like the code of behavior as part of their daily life. Yet it is critical, day to day, moment to moment, that we exercise self-awareness. When the function of accepting and rejecting values is left to the subconscious, the results are based on chance – pretty sloppy for such an important part of determining who we are. For example, whether we believe or disbelieve something can be a critical, sensitive and an important decision yet we may allow it to take place without proper forethought.

My favorite saying regarding the matter of self-awareness is, "if you don't see it or hear it, it never happened." It is important to note that the humans have five senses which are see, hear, taste, Touch and Smell. There is one unofficial sense which is seldom talked about, and that is Common Sense. Now in the matter of Awareness the most frequently used are Seeing, Hearing and Common Sense. So if you are in a state of self-awareness, you are seriously paying attention to the information available to you by focusing on these three. That is a big part of the Starting Search for Reality.

Along with this matter I always bring in the issue of the Functional Hypocrite. This philosophy says that people automatically become Functional Hypocrites with their professor at school, with their boss on the job, as well as with people that are generally about. This principle demands conciliatory behavior when required and there are many situations where this is required. Therefore the individual must possess self-awareness in order to determine the need for the Functional Hypocrite Model. The latter is a matter of values that for the most part is an automatic response although impossible to ignore. This latter situation is an extension of the activity of self-awareness and a desire to Get Along.

In addition to my lectures and in my management activities I always bring to the attention of my associates the nature of Robinson's Law, which says, "think up front and live easy." The philosophy recognizes that a relaxed life which is acceptable to most can only occur if you think up front, constantly; that is the essence of self-awareness. As a result of living easy, happiness prevails and so does personal comfort - which is a boon to peace and tranquility while living the American Dream. So it is important to recognize that for the good life the issue of values which must be managed. The issue works in many strata and among many attitudes. Proficiency is a critical element, which is highly connected with the management of one's values such that self-esteem is never sacrificed. The worst is to compromise values which are directly related to self-esteem, self-worth and self-respect, the Three Fabulous Synonyms. So please remember throughout life: Think up front and live easy.

CHAPTER 7. THE POWER OF REALITY

The issue of Reality today is a rare talking point among Americana. Yet this principle is the most critical aspect when we begin to think about the art of coping with life. The subject of Reality in practice is a total mystery to most folks. Therefore this chapter offering the power of Reality serves the reader in an extremely helpful category. Reality is the way things really are. The problem occurs in its absence, when behavior and decisions are a shot in the dark. We should always try to avoid making such random reactions. If you behave according to Reality, you are most likely to be correct.

So every day the individual must identify the Reality at hand in order to proceed to the conclusion with minimum stress. In some situations, it's obvious what is needed, while others require in-depth awareness. The most important element is to always be in the frame of reference whereby you take a moment of internal concentration to be sure you have recognized Reality. The nature of this proposition should be part of one's Awareness of life and ability to cope.

People absolutely need to maintain a conscious useful state regarding the subject of Reality. If not, then confusing and erroneous behavior will be a constant problem. Negativisms and poor decisions should be avoided. Unfortunately America is constantly searching for peace and happiness but obviously most people have no idea how to get there. How to cope with Reality is generally not in practice; actually, most of what we see and read in the news and entertainment media are cast precisely so as to confuse us about what is real.

Thus people constantly respond automatically, with negativisms and emotions I call the Bias Phenomenon. They constantly duel, unfortunately in a dangerous, poorly understood phenomenon. Even though the majority of people are seeking the same thing: a tranquil and fulfilling life – they have minimal success in the current questionable environment. All of America hase a need and should be awarded a new vista of peace and happiness.

That which I am about to discuss will offer confused people a beneficial and encouraging alternative. In general the word Reality appears on and off throughout this entire book. It is an extremely powerful word for all levels of humanity. It is the difference between a near-perfect life and mediocrity. It is an open door to achieving the American Dream. Unfortunately, the question of Reality continues to fall into a category of a mystery. Reality continues too frequently as an unknown and not part of Awareness and unfortunately lies in an unconscious helpless State. Bias is the undesirable substitute.

Comprehension of Reality should be available as a creative asset. When there is a constant feeling of inadequacy the only outcome is Tension. Until we have comprehension and control, peace and happiness will be missing. Unfortunately, most people do not have access to any guidance about this.

Every human being has a Value System, good or bad, though may of us are not conscious of the values our actions reflect. As part of a process of maturity, and thereafter, every human being adopts a system of values, often automatically or subconsciously. To the reader I say, "have you recently reviewed your value inventory?" Of course the answer most likely will be only a blank face. Most people hae never given it a thought. Yet values are what control your behavior and the process is critical. You are under this influence and yet the common practice is to be totally unaware of this Reality.

A few examples of values are as follows. Concern for others, Courtesy, Honesty, and Being Helpful, Truthful, Aware,

Ambitious, Cooperative, Inquisitive, and Taking Care of Family. Are these values part of your inventory? Are there other qualities that you actually value more? Make a list, and go over it from time to time; see if your thinking has changed. (Obviously this question is unfair for the majority. Before answering the question, the party must possess self-awareness, which is also unknown to the majority.) Many people are behaving under the banner of "running wild." The value system issue is available to all members of society and the nature of your inventory should be a matter of your Concern and Awareness. It appears that the young in particular are totally ignorant on the matter, but when you look at their elders, you may conclude they are not doing any better.

Awareness

As a further study to the subject of Reality, I will commence with the issue of Awareness. Awareness is a constant active fundamental characteristic within the human as a facilitator. Yet as a conscious, daily issue, it is my observation that most people do not welcome such reflection. Awareness is when you are conscious of all that is taking place within your space. If you do not see it or hear it, it never happened. So it is reasonable to attach Reality to your being while hearing or seeing; they add up to Awareness. If you decipher Reality through Hearing and Seeing, obviously your behavioral pattern will be much improved.

The model is to be constantly considering information by virtue of your ability to Hear and See while developing Awareness. This statement is more or less obvious but it is hardly recognized by many. If you are a person of high level Awareness, then your resultant life should be filled with peace and happiness. At the same time we can say that if you are highly Self-Aware you are prepared to decipher Reality accurately.

The topic of Decision Making falls under the banner of self-awareness. The first element of decision making is to be sure that you have all the facts. The latter is made available through self-awareness and digging. Believe it or not, decision making consists of deciphering Reality first. If you do not have all the facts, then decision making relies on the unholy Gut Feeling. But that, in truth, is making a decision based on anything but Reality and it is dangerous. The level of accuracy in gut-feeling decisions is highly dependent on whether the situation under consideration falls within your past experience. When such a situation arises and an immediate decision is required, and there is no time to obtain the facts and utilize your Self-Awareness, then obviously you must take a shot in the dark. Hopefully, you can find something in your past experiences to at least start you in the right direction.

This is where Common Sense comes into play. In some ways, it is more valuable than the five official senses. The recommendation is to never forget to utilize Common Sense to super impose over the two senses of See and Hear. This warning is to offer further caution in developing the reality that you are about to study and make decisions. Common Sense tells us that we should take a serious review and decipher Reality from all points of questions so that you commence your analysis on a sound basis.

800 A Minute – A Case History

At this point I am reminded of a case history early in my career. I was working as an engineer whereby the company had just installed a production line for their number one product, and it was designed for 800 units a minute. No matter what was tried, the solution of 800 a minute was a mystery. No member of the organization was able to solve the problem. I was given the assignment. As I witnessed the operation in order to obtain all the facts I had to sit, observe and record for approximately two weeks. Eventually, observed Reality told me the solution as follows. I call this Reaction to Reality "The facts talked back to me." When machine number 7 out of 8 went down, for instance, machines 1 through 6 waited and this phenomenon would occur through the entire shift, causing various increments of lost time. So the facts alerted me to a solution, which was to make machines 1 through 8 operative more often. Thus the question was as follows. If machines 1 through 8 had a place to store semi-finished product, when the line started up they could add those pieces in small increments onto the conveyers, converting this semi-finished product by slipping it onto the line. After a meeting or two with the employees, we made box trucks for the partially finished product to be stored at every machine. When any machines interrupted the work flow, the other stations upstream could continue producing semi-finished goods to be placed in the box trucks. Later, as the opportunity presented itself, they slipped into the line the semi-finished product and made up for lost time. In two weeks they were producing 800 a minute. This case history is a good example of philosophy number one in decision making: obtain all the facts. Gut feeling is the last resort. The facts talked back to me with reality.

In this particular case history a number of people had tried to find a solution, but without seeing and observing all of the facts they were unable to solve the problem. I worked in corporate row for 43 years and I can assure you that I never forgot that exercise, where I avoided going by Gut Feeling but took the seemingly more time-consuming - yet eventually successful - route. The major factor is that my self-awareness in the onset told me that I must take the time to observe and study the situation until "the facts talked back to me."

Another aspect of Awareness is that it brings forth consciousness regarding your self-worth. If you have a high level of self-worth, you will always judge the correctness of your behavior whereby you refuse to sacrifice any portion of your self-worth, self-esteem or self-respect. Since all of these three are basically the same, I have labeled them the Three Fabulous Synonyms. The individual maintains good impressions of himself by judging his behavioral pattern in accordance with his self-worth and value system.

When a person makes an honest decision, it is the Value System that prevails. However, if values are of no concern, then the entire formula breaks down. In my daily work as a leader, I always came to conclusions as conscientiously indicated by my value system. My self-worth has always been extremely important to me and my behavior always reflected that restraint. It is difficult for me to overlook the negatives that I see in others so as a result I achieved a favorable status.

It is my sincere belief that negative values, or a lack of values have infiltrated the attitudes of many of our citizens and it is reflected in the behavior our current culture. For example KKK, Neo Nazis, and White Supremacists, as well as those who fight for the right to promote illegal immigration – to promote breaking a law that was designed to protect our country - are among us and they publicly demonstrate. Our sovereignty is threatened as our population and our ability to pay for all the government-funded programs are overwhelmed by the increasing number of illegal arrivals. The foregoing is only the tip of the iceberg, and President Trump is being hindered, obstructed and insulted every time he even opens his mouth about it. How can a country function when the citizens no longer respect national anthem and the Constitution which maintains their freedom, no longer respect federal law, and refuse to allow the elected president to do his job?

It is difficult to comprehend how so many people have lost their recognition of Reality, which means that they have lost their way. Our only hope is to support our current leadership regardless of all the attempts to discredit him. Currently value systems are a far cry from a reasonable, conscious evaluation of Reality and along with the sad state of the compromising self-esteem. The sad facts cannot be ignored.

Drugs

Is marijuana harmless? It appears that the number of deadly car accidents has increased noticeably in states where marijuana has been made legal. Is there a relationship? Is this an example of "change for the sake of change" or is it that corporations are more interested in making a huge profit than in keeping the population safe? The same question can be applied to all types of products, from cell phones and radiation to weed killers and cancer. The rapid nature of change in our culture is creating insecurity, whereby people are still ignorant and unaware of the basic question. It is my sincere hope that all that I record will cause the individual to stop and take notice and evaluate what is occurring to the culture of the United States. The government is not getting involved, except where there is an obvious question involving law or politics. On the whole, the characteristics of the Facial Hair and Cleavage Culture illustrate superficial, poorly-considered, uncomplicated and meaningful change. Very serious matters are totally ignored. There is little understanding of the characteristics of this movement and there is no unified activity to attempt to bring it under control. Of course negatives do prevail such as riots, violence, degradation of the police; and where this will end is a great question. It is my claim that all that is occurring as a result of our culture is a problem where the majority do not have comprehension to raise the questions for solution. Consequently the New Culture is well on the way, flourishing and problematic.

For example, does the culture improve my life or my family's life? Are the real aspects of Facial Hair and Cleavage anything positive? Are the present music and entertainment trends designed for profit only? Culture used to be that which cultivates what's best in humanity.

In order to analyze the situation, people must understand how to pause, calling on Awareness and Reality, in order to come to logical, healthy conclusions. The latter would possibly reject the vapidity of our existing culture.

Of course the primary solution is to think through one's values and behavior, and to keep those thoughts in mind. We need to recognize that today's culture truly does not promote an improved, honorable American life. The power of Reality is ignored, consequently the power of choice is ignored and the true value of life is subdued by the absence of Awareness and Reality. The result is a very tense insecure populace.

We have in a number of ways related to our culture where reality, positiveness and change are at opposite ends of the spectrum. The unawareness of America does not promote questioning the nature of our culture. It more so responds to the demands of change for the sake of change, without reason or value. It is my observation that the majority ignore Reality completely; so consequently it has been my objective to teach the understanding of the concepts which offer the individual a more conscious, alternate point of open view. A great deal of the culture is basically a movement that is confusing. The latter brings forth complete ignorance on the matter of Reality to the majority. Change for the sake of change usually equals zero, if not a step bckwards.

So often the necessary Reality is by no means a part of Awareness which only promotes superficiality and tension. The formula is simply "what you see is what you get" and meaningless thought without any inner consideration. There is no argument. There is no sensibility and worse there is no Reality. I do believe that people who lived in the 40s and 50s have memories of a strong, tight American culture that was highly identifiable. It became real since the populace was deciphering Reality, a discriminating group. Consequently planning and intelligence influenced choice of change. The current state accepts superficialities that truly do not improve the path to peace and happiness. It is my objective to teach life involving Reality and how to cope. Reality awaits on your door step. Be aware, with Robinson's Law, and daily "Think upfront and live easy." Reality is on your doorstep - Don't trip.

CHAPTER 8. ONE PLUS ONE IS EQUAL TO ONE

In an unsatisfactory culture, you might expect that marriage would be a problematic area. Obviously that is the case in America and throughout Western society. The basic problem is that love and marriage are no longer synonymous. Under a state of tension and in a poorly understood culture, it seems logical that such a negative exists causing a great deal of unhappiness. From a coping point of view, people are no longer adept at creating a positive marriage, which develops from a primary state of a negative culture that is poorly qualified and not understood. Simply said, it's a sign of a falling culture.

Marriage can provide a safe haven if the members of the duo are people who have a high level of success in coping. Since most people are not well equipped to cope, it is no surprise that divorce has reached epic proportions in a falling empire. Tension follows tension and such matters create insecurity and other negatives. It is very simple to further the event into marital unhappiness. So therefore it is by no means a surprise under the Facial hair and Cleavage Culture that we declare one more category in conflict which creates the marriage mania.

This chapter primarily will offer a series of coping techniques to find peace and tranquility for marriages as well as all other types of conflict. For example during the courting period two people are under their best behavior and when they marry, they are two strangers with a great deal of coping necessary to ameliorate inadequate understandings of each other. Chapter 8 devotes its entire span to solving this 50 percent mania. The primary effort is coping with Reality while becoming fully aware of one's reality.

The title of this chapter, "One Plus One Is Equal To One," is a philosophical truism that develops when peace and happiness are at the core of marriage. For example, I can attest that over time, in happiness the couples perform a tremendous activity to meet each other's needs. When the principle mutual objective is to maintain a constant feeling of receptivity, an inner "smiling face," two people become one. That is what forms the base for maintaining and optimizing matrimony.

During courting and further on, both parties must be in a constant awareness for each other's personalities. This situation requires a procedure that I have labeled Conversational Analysis. The primary aspect of this procedure is to maintain a high level Awareness of all interactions within the couple. This is tantamount to long term success. You must constantly evaluate with awareness the meaning of the full recognition of the conversation. The rest is common sense. At a later point we'll follow up on the details to determine the overall style of your partner.

The more you learn about your partner as a result of Conversational Analysis, the more accurate will be your prediction about the future. If you wish to take written notes of your experience following a get-together, it is certainly a valuable idea since it is also critical after each experience to evaluate the results. If things don't go well, the contrariness can be estimated as a percentage and if the latter is beyond the 60 percent mark for negatives, you must think twice before pursuing the relationship. Exploratory discussions are necessary for understanding the couple's personalities. It is also to create a change from two complete strangers to a state whereby compatible personality and traits readily become a subject for your consideration and evaluation.

One Plus One Equals One

Unfortunately, love and marriage are broken. Obviously, when love evaporates, the remainder is a battlefield which ends up in a divorce, which causes major destruction of each person's security, tranquility, and not to be under-estimated, financial well-being. Certainly the entire event does not promote peace and happiness, which are required to achieve longevity. Stress is at a maximum and the continuing painful memories over-write the soothing, happy memories of the time when things were going well; this creates sadness and tension overtime. It appears that a majority of couples could use some assistance with their basic guidelines of marriage and life. There is no rulebook of instructions that would simplify the matter. It requires dedication and work on the part of both parties.

That being said, the rules for providing solutions are not difficult to comprehend and make a lot of sense. They work. Regardless of whether you are already married, courting, or single and fancy free, all that I record I guarantee will work in all of these categories and provide immediate enlightenment. So go ahead and Get it Right the First Time.

The method of coping comes in at the top of the list in ensuring successful marital process. Remember, the coping process demands behavior according to your best values set, in spite of opposing pressures. Self-awareness plus positivism is the correct formula under all conditions. Tension and cultural disparity is the culprit.

What you will learn are solutions that have worked for me for more than half a century. If your marriage is overburdened with conflict, anger and dissatisfaction, you are ready to become a statistic. Stop, take a deep breath, calm down and allow the content of this chapter to turn the tables to happiness. For sure, divorce is a frequent invader in our overall failing culture. It does not have to reach the danger point if you take seriously this content. Read on and consider the advice with the foreknowledge that these tactics have been tested and retested for more than a half of a century with blissful results. It is time to eliminate the skirmishes, heal the wounds and overcome the negatives that make marriage precarious. Unfortunately, there is a beginning and end to everything, and most important when the day of parting arrives is that the marriage survivor can say with solemn certainty, no regrets, no regrets.

During my long marriage, we were constantly challenged, tested by the objective, taunted by moments of misgiving, only to overcome and preserve our tender love. May your marriage be as good as mine.

A lot of it comes down to learning to apply the technique called Conversational Analysis. This approach should be part of constant Awareness before, during and after the entire marriage. During this analysis a high level of correction is a necessity. The critical period is during the courting era since during that phase, everyone generally recognizes that the objective is to be on one's best behavior, and it is relatively easy to show one's "good" side for a short while, keeping negative traits relatively in check. This can, however, result in two complete strangers standing at the altar in the process of reciting their vows.

The purpose of Conversational Analysis is to fully take advantage of the verbal interchange as an important predictor of a successful marriage. For example, during courtship you may notice that your partner has mud on his or her shoes. So you comment to your partner, "Your shoes are muddy," and the response is, "So what?" At a later moment you mention that you're unhappy there's so much violence in the movies. The response is, "That's what makes them great." A third example would be, "I love to cook," and the response is "I prefer to eat out." If you are not paying attention, such reactions will not register and after marriage they will multiply, quickly becoming an issue of disparity and tension. So Conversational Analysis is a critical application which should be carefully introduced as part of the ongoing interactions of the courting period and beyond. Too much disparity provides a complicated barrier to peace and happiness and stands in the way of movement towards longevity. It is important to question the responses while observing the level of flexibility in your partner. A danger sign is when your partner demonstrates an inability to handle criticism.

Beyond all other factors, the overall value system of each partner will make or break the pathway of marriage. A critical long term characteristic of successful marriage is that the value systems of both parties become compatible. In fact, the human value system is an inventory of ingrained behavioral characteristics that identifies the individual. This inventory identifies your overall personality and behavioral style. During the interactions between the partners, opinions will be expressed that demonstrate important values. In the overall scheme of things, the action of values is a daily occurrence between the partners. Then the objective should be to negotiate values until both parties are highly acceptable to each other's inventory.

Patriotism, the news and politics are the type of issues that need negotiating. Consequently there is a litany of giveaway responses made that are assuredly subject to recognition by constant awareness. Unless the latter is in play, there is no true understanding of each other. So when interacting, maintain a high level Awareness of behavior and conversation with your partner. This requires concentrated application during the courting period and as necessary during the marriage. Eventually, both parties take on a spirit of relaxation and automatic receptivity with comfort and expectation that both parties are on the right track. When this state is achieved, there is a likelihood that these couples are living in peace and happiness, in the expectation that mutual understanding prevails and it is time to relax. The question of divorce is out of view, and peace and harmony are in.

Also One Plus One Equals One is in force. Needless to say, if both parties are willing to negotiate values, there is a high prediction of long term success. The latter procedure is an extension of Conversational Analysis. However, if one member refuses the above, walk away. Flexibility in both members is critical. Throughout this process persuasion and compromise should be in play constantly.

At this point it seems proper to offer a case history to demonstrate the value of Conversational Analysis during courting and beyond. This case history is as follows. Mrs. Beverly Bravo tells Mrs. Lady Luck that her lady friend has a son who would like to meet someone suitable for dating. Lady told her daughter, Lily Lovely, who is very positive, and the deal is made. Bill Bravo calls her and they go out for dinner.

Lily wears her best attire and perfume and Bill comes in everyday jeans and a T-shirt. He also has an untrimmed 5-day beard. Is it planned or by chance? That evening they chat over many unimportant subjects and there are observations as follows. Bill orders three cocktails before dinner and is a bit brusque with the waitress. His shoes are dirty and occasionally four letter words slip out. It so happens that he is studying to be a surgeon.

They have a second meeting and it goes just about the same way. They are comfortable with each other and find it a pleasure to communicate. At this point, it is important to recognize that there are fundamentally two types of value sets. For example, Bill does not like Lily's hairstyle or her hair color, but he doesn't say so. At the same level of concentration, Lily recognizes two important negatives. She finds it obnoxious to be confronted with Bill's muddy shoes. She is also annoyed with Bill's roughness towards the waitress. In time, there will be open discussion regarding these things. Problems should not be left unattended.

In this Case History these two potential lovers avoid discussions of differences until they both say "I do," which is typical. No doubt this is only the tip of the iceberg. Yet full interaction has not occurred. Marriage takes place and both parties return from the honeymoon. Unfortunately this case history repeats itself often. The internal characteristics continue to stay undercover while the externals are not addressed even though they are observed.

Typically as husband and wife there is a constant movement and modification, with interactions that include negotiating values. In this case, the two parties are overwhelmed with the pleasure of the association and they immediately and naturally commence negotiating values for their betterment. The process of these negotiations is persuasion and compromise. Both parts of these interactions require a full courteous interchange on a daily basis.

Eventually the process is in play with less effort and stress, on a daily basis, and gradually the marriage becomes an excellent example of what can be achieved in spite of a complicated beginning. The success of the marriage is a motivation above and beyond which automatically invites the process of persuasion and compromise in a sophisticated, respectful level, bringing the matter closer and closer to correctness. It can be done in spite of the poor beginning. A great deal depends on a sincerity of two individuals willing to negotiate and modify.

Throughout this case history there was an important phenomenon in play as follows. Specifically each person in the duo used all 5 senses plus common sense. As well, applying the rule "If you don't see it or hear it, it never happened" is a major advantage and technique in courting and marriage. There must be a constant search for Reality in order to promote favorable change. The door then opens to peace, happiness in marriage and aids overtime in achieving longevity. This analysis is an important base for the utilization of Awareness in finding Mutual Understanding and compatibility for the couple, an important enlightenment to the couple pro and con while engaging in Conversational Analysis.

At this juncture I wish to offer four interesting episodes of research that brought about many of the convictions that I have described throughout.

Case History 1

The Troy, New York, Community College called me to discuss an opportunity. They wanted to put together a class of rank and file individuals, namely fork truck operators, construction workers and tradesmen. The assignment was to teach these people to develop awareness and high level consciousness for Reality. I accepted the responsibility and we advertised, and approximately 30 individuals signed on.

These workers had never been exposed to the power of Reality. We had a program for approximately for one full semester which covered three months. We covered items such as the meaning of self-esteem, a conscious value that all people must respect, contain and never compromise, the feature of Reality. We also covered the idea that "If you don't see it or hear it, it never happened." We went over the five senses and the all-important addition, common sense, which enable one to become more accurate in behavior, while being more relaxed and more aware.

With Awareness you can decipher Reality successfully,

moving toward the goal of peace and happiness, thus increasing the chances of enjoying a long and healthy life.

While teaching and studying this experience, I brought in Robinson's Law, which the class appreciated tremendously: "Think up front and live easy." A typical striking phrase that attracts attention and awareness within itself.

At the end of this experience the Community College asked me to become the Dean of the Management School (which would have made me happy, but I was already fully committed). The entire class presented me with a plaque that they all had signed and the major statement listed is Robinson's Law. My work in this case showed that rank and file workers can find great value in material that is not taught to the general public.

The major issues are awareness and adjustability, which are critical for the work environment as well as the marital experience. The data indicates that all the above can be learned with determination. Consequently "One Plus One Equals One" will take place more frequently within this group as a matter of everyday life. Hopefully this exposure will offer an opportunity for the class members to move up in management. These techniques can be learned by all levels of society, whereby the result will deserve to be called Impeccable Behavior.

Case History 2

In this particular case I was teaching a group of potential officers at West Point. Every time I entered the classroom, somebody yelled "Attention" (in fact, it came across as "tension"!) and all the students, aged about 40, jumped to their feet and stood at attention. I walked to my desk, turned around and said loudly, "As you were, gentlemen," and the students relaxed and sat at their desks. Nobody ever fell asleep or showed signs of boredom, and they were totally the best students I have ever experienced. Apparently West Point had heard of my work and wanted their officers to learn Awareness plus. I must say it was the most attentive, genteel group of motivated individuals that I had ever worked with. I can assure you that in future activities these gentlemen will recite a prayer and it will be Robinson's Law. A strong experience that defines a willingness to accept change and the veracity of the material.

Case History 3

In this example the purpose of the research was Objectivity Training of production supervisors. I would present a case problem which needed to be solved. As part of the training in awareness, etc., I explained to the 20 plus supervisors that there was only one solution. Individually, they had to decipher this solution as a part of their examination. The question was, Is it possible for some 20 individuals to arrive at the same true answer where there is only one result acceptable? In time, we proved that Awareness will decipher the right solution. The purpose that is determined is that Awareness and Reality provide solutions even when a multiplicity of humans are working on the same problem. Reality recognition is the major objective. I also received a very complimentary plaque from these supervisor students. The experiment to uncover one solution and one Reality by using self-awareness is an important aid in leadership and managing. Objectivity can be identical between two or more individuals if Reality prevails.

Case History 4

On several occasions I was the senior operating officer of several enterprises involving thousands of individuals. Needless to say, every day was not only a work day but also was a research day. I have PE after my name since I qualified in Civil, Mechanical, Electrical, Chemical and Industrial Engineering, PE means Professional Engineer. My staff were aware of this qualification and whenever a problem arose, they called me instead of the engineering department. I taught all the supervisors how to perform a basic engineering analysis – which is actually a true function of self-awareness.

This technique required the supervisors to find the total definition of the problem before they called me, and in some cases they were able to recommend solutions. Obviously I wanted accurate analysis and definition so that we could come to a reasonable and immediate conclusion. This developed a supervisory organization that was impervious and adept at finding Reality in a singular specialized approach. I used to tell this group that I expected only impeccable behavior. This study showed that Reality knows no limitation and can facilitate the achievement of impeccable behavior among a group of production supervisors. In fact the supervisors became adept at exercising their awareness and search for Reality in generalized problem solving.

In finality, we understand and comprehend the title 1+1=1, whereby the complication of inadequacy during the courting period is overcome and marriage is according to our recommendations. We also highlight the technique of Conversational Analysis and its relative Awareness as mandatory characteristics for peace and happiness, while striving for Impeccable Behavior and additionally while implementing Robinson's Law. In various venues and with various types of individuals, the basic principles of Awareness and Reality were demonstrated in their variety and veracity. Divorce is a sign of, and a cause of tremendous stress; likewise, job failure. This commentary teaches you how to avoid both maladies. The success to longevity is based on minimal stress and achievement of peace and happiness.

During courting you recognize differences in opinions, beliefs etc., with your partner. The question during this experience is, does my partner appear to be flexible, and open to different ideas – and am I flexible and open? It is always proper to discuss differences and determine flexibility. This way, intolerance becomes a nasty word and when it is present, complications will arise. I would encourage all parties to devote considerable time to come to proper understanding on such matters. The more you do, the better the marriage with longevity.

As a final thought to this chapter, I wish you a marriage that is as loving, supportive and caring as mine.

Attaining peace and happiness is the proper path to longevity. I am sincerely convinced that all that I present without doubt is a door opener that I have personally experienced leading to my attainment of 95 years young. Please be aware what has been offered herein and gain the objectives that we have outlined.

In a substrata cultural environment, it is very possible that marriage will become a very difficult issue above and beyond. The process of coping under the vigor of a falling cultural state will certainly put additional pressure on the 50 percent of marriages that do, so far, survive. With time, however, it would not be a surprise to see the situation respond to proper coping. The problem is that the pressure of an inadequate culture has its effect; yet with the techniques of coping that we have proposed, the candidates may be able to take on a mature and relaxed view of marriage and its future.

Hence all that we say in the effort to correct America's failure is intended to overcome the negatives of the unsatisfactory culture. This in turn would have a positive effect on marriage rates. All that is included in this chapter leading to impeccable behavior, and for the most part the technique of Coping is generally applicable throughout.

Chapter 9. Coping - The Game Plan Of Life

At this juncture I wish to in finality move to the heart of coping for my readers. I use this terminology regarding the heart of coping where there is at present a tremendous vapidity in life. Throughout this book I have discussed all of the issues regarding this topic. I have included methodology, discussions and clarity of application. However I wish to take the final step to providing the application of coping by offering extensive finalized commentary that provides a bold summary that facilitates super application as follows. I leave no stones unturned and at times through repetition offer extensive clarification for a difficult subject.

Offer I repeat a principle in several locations to develop in depth comprehension to the entire complexity of Facial Hair and Cleavage Culture. This strategy once again is designed to allow consideration of various aspects relative to new items in future chapters. So therefore the reader becomes multifaceted. The nature of coping is found in several purposes and therefore we need comprehension in all those purposes. Hence the repetitive strategy. Read On.

Reality

The first topic is Reality which applies to every possible

facet in life. The primary objective is to decipher and search for true Reality in every matter of the day to day. After you have deciphered from an absolute mess the description of Reality will bring you much closed to the definition of a solution. Certainly your Resulting Reality Behavior will be more accurate. An uncomplicated rule applicable to all matters. Eventually this response becomes habitual and helpful.

Without this forethought, your ensuing behavior as applied could be an error and heading for failure. The opposite of Reality is Bias, which is simply a failure to reach a correct understanding of reality and reacting instead through gut feelings. Emotion without reasoning, and without pondering the input from your five senses and common sense, will lead to poor decisions; that is, failure. When you decipher reality, it must be clearly the truth where you have recognized possible interference of bias, which you must set aside immediately. In order to fully describe this phenomenon I wish to take a case history from my inventory which we shall call for a better name the Reality Orientation.

Case History 1. The Reality Orientation

Early in my career I was assigned the job of making the warehouse, shipping departments and storage more efficient. I was told all kind of stories as follows. This department was the "toughest" in the entire business. Was large enough to require a full building with proper docks, etc., and labeled with the underground management comment that the complete area was off grounds for a management person.

The latter turned out to be a fact. There were bulletins posted that stated Stan Robinson would enter the floor on such and such date for the commencement of a total overall study of this area. I was told, off the record, that I should wear a bullet proof vest and, further, that most of the employees carried a weapon-style knife. But don't forget that I had just returned from World War II with the US Navy, spending over three years on the high seas in a killer environment.

So on my first day while I was standing alone, a vicious, belligerent type walked up to me with the question, "How would you like to have your throat cut"? It turned out that this individual was a chief steward of the union. I made a quick decision to respond in accordance with the reality. And my retort was as follows: "If you take a look at my throat, you will notice a few scars where they tried but failed to do the job." The union steward shook my hand with an attitudinal, powerful feeling that said, "You're one of us." He shook my hand and smiled and turned out to be a wonderful friend.

I took the time on every assignment to provide a prior explanation so that he could tell his associates that he had approved all my projects in advance. Otherwise, I do believe that I would have been escorted outside the warehouse and told to go to the office building.

Every time I started a project, I met with the steward. Whenever I entered a new area in the shipping warehousing department, I was happy to find this steward bringing me up to date on what I was about to do so that he could serve as my public relations manager.

During my entire assignment to that area, which I would call the "wild side," I was met with difficult positions, attitudes, questions and in all cases I stood forthright, with respect and peace. I must say that whenever I commenced a project I was always told the truth by the union personnel. I responded the same way and was accepted by all members of the union. I never tried to avoid them. In fact, in all cases I achieved the position of reality all to my favor.

The several months I worked solely in that department, making sure that the work load was proper, efficient and that all matters pertaining to work were carefully studied from the employees' point of view. In fact I would review with the union my recommendations prior to making a presentation to management. The rank and file in many cases were more diligent about reality than I was. My whole relation with the workers was one of practicing reality in all matters. The latter was the key to my success. Therefore when I made a presentation to management regarding my activities, I made sure that the rank and file got the credit they deserved for cooperation, in advance important information and guidance which was based on fairness and all other avenues of deciphering reality. I maintained a high position from my workers including respect, honesty and concern for the workers' well-being.

Thus, the introductory "Would you like to have your throat cut" was forgotten, based on my behavior in making sure that all matters were submitted in reality and the bias was carefully excluded. The proposition of reality was clearly the entrance to trust, friendliness, being communicative etc., which was the preamble for all of my activities. My first six month at that position concluded without a single grievance.

The next time you are accosted with the question, "How would you like to have your throat cut?" understand that, translated, it really means you are in complete accord with the rank and file in the effort to decipher reality, which otherwise could be a war zone. The above was a truly a bold search for Reality and a protecting device that served to my benefit several years thereafter. In fact, I was invited to the union Christmas Party, which is usually off limits because after a few drinks someone could find himself struggling with a desire to beat up a management person. This interaction could be considered, since this group was the toughest. As always Reality is the way things really are, i.e., the truth and can serve the individual in a lifetime of success.

Now a final commentary to the subject of Reality. This subject is a clinical problem that I have labeled with "you are not alone." The latter situation arises when you and another individual have different descriptions of the same reality.

For example your boss, teacher, or a policeman could be your opponent. In this situation, let's call it R - R¹, your Reality R is in conflict with the boss's, for example. His Reality, I have labeled R¹. In order to overcome this complication, it becomes necessary to assume the role of the functional hypocrite. This role could serve as your way to avoid complications, i.e., R¹. You must become expert in performing this role and utilize conciliatory behavior to satisfy the boss. The complication arises when achieving the same reality for both parties is necessary. The functional hypocrite must appear to be with accord while achieving unison of either one or the other realities. This comes about through negotiations and can be a critical technique to retaining peace with the boss but yet it is necessary to understand which reality is applicable and by no means a simple chore. You need to be a sales person.

The Culture

Culture is the social behavior and norms found in human societies. The arts and other manifestations of human intellectual achievement regarded collectively. Culture is the way of life of a particular people, especially as shown in their ordinary behavior and habits, their attitudes toward each other, and their moral and religious beliefs. For sure coping is the game plan of life and critically important area. You must comprehend the nature and effect of the culture. More important recognize the unfavorable effects to your life. The above list is a pretty basic definition for the word culture. All of these definitions seem to purport the idea that your personal life style is influenced by a response to the nature of the environment. So therefore you respond to norms in your environment, as manifestations of human intellect.

It can be said that your style of behavior is heavily influenced by the nature of your environment. So then why do I call this the Facial Hair and Cleavage Culture? If we follow the definition, both characterizations somewhere along the line came to a conclusion that sporting facial hair and revealing cleavage were necessary modifications, considering the environment. Most people seem not to have any conscious idea why they are doing it. It is my belief that both Facial Hair and Cleavage are firstly a way of affiliating with a group, providing some sort of security and comfort. It's a way of disregarding the negatives of the existing culture. But this does nothing to address the real problem.

A Major Step: Values

In all venues Coping is a valuable asset. After a baby is born, he or she is nurtured with food, sleep and love. As time passes, the little one begins to respond to values. If you sing a song, the child will enjoy and attach the value of singing to their inventory of values.

All of this activity takes place generally with minimum attention and complications. One could say that this particular activity is carried out in an undesirable style. It is important to note that the child becomes a young adult in a state of relaxation and is not aware of his value set. If you ask young people to describe their value sets, most would respond with a question, "What are you talking about?"

Yet every mode of behavior that you execute is probably covered by a value. In most cases you have opportunity regarding the situation at hand and selecting a proper response. Unfortunately selecting values becomes an automatic activity "done and finished," moving on to the next situation. As already stated I can quickly reiterate to you a group of values that I call my number one battery as follows. The role of a person at 95 is one who provides his family and associates with a value system that is based on family, God, heritage, caring, courtesy, wisdom, love and patriotism. The latter is just a sampling of my value set that is a conscious part of my Reality. Therefore when I face a situation in society I can actually take a few seconds to carefully select suitable, responsive values.

What is the first objective? (1) I must be behaving in accordance with Codes of Behavior that reflect recognizable values as guiding factors. Being reality oriented is synonymous with being Value Oriented. (2)So therefore since most of the citizens do not consciously think in that manner whereby such knowledge and practice can be of tremendous aid in responding to the Facial Hair and Cleavage Culture.

For example America is tense. There are a great number of "wrongs" in our present culture. This creates a state of unstable effects on ones attitude. A better condition would be whereby you would never have to face such complications. The question arises how I can avoid the negative on so many fronts. What shall I do? "The facial hair and cleavage culture" creates discomfort and tension without an obvious method of avoidance.

There is a condition whereby the culture constantly continues to grow. The latter requires a preoccupation whereby the individual gives serious thought to the negatives of the culture. The question must arise what is wrong with our present culture.

Coping

Decipher reality constantly; execute your value system to regulate a behavior pattern that makes you feel more comfortable as part of coping.

1. Recognize Reality and all of the negatives. Be sure that your value system is suitable to deal with the culture presumable negative. Oppose each of the undesirable conditions in your reality by selecting the values that will give you the greatest amount of comfort.

The values you select should provide you with comprehension, sympathy although some of the negatives are better of avoided. The problem is that most people do not manage their value system consciously; they completely overlook the fact that is there waiting to be utilized in coping with the negatives of the culture. So once again examine the elements of the culture and with further reality orientation utilize the proper values to find comfort in opposition. You will openly recognize your tension in a state of subsiding. If everyone follows this methodology, America will be Great Again.

Chapter 10. Pros And Cons

There is an old adage that frequently used to be recited in Big Business:

"If you can't produce the product right, don't try to sell it."

I devoted my whole career to big business and have learned to take full heed in order to be successful. I might add that I was devoted to this adage and I was successful.

Unfortunately and obviously our federal government is primarily staffed with individuals that would not qualify to be hired in big business and this adage is unknown to them.

Quality is a subliminal message. When the quality message is experienced the customer is mesmerized to return and further purchase the product. That experience occurs constantly time and time again. Remember that production and quality are compatible profiles. At this point I will further explain. Quality must be the first order of manufacturing of a product. Marketing so often a practical profession recommends a goal of 97 percent as a working statistic. As the senior operations executive I have always strived for a hundred percent in quality in all matters including life. Therefore in daily practice I have refined the Adage to my point of view. I have achieved and overcome this principle while always maintaining a one hundred percent requirement on Quality plus. The fundamental principal is that I refuse to surrender to the adage and have been successful accordingly in Business and Life. Furthermore I have been always provided security and dignity to the Rank and File presumably the American way.

I relate this tale since I have always utilized the discussion to the Quality of Life which is my forte and experience. Most of my experience has been concerned with providing products with a 100 percent quality and living personally in an equal manner. This effort is constantly discussed from many points of view in my writing and the achievement of 95 Years Young. This entire book has been a discussion exemplified by the constant objective of 100 percent Quality in Life. So many situations are discussed along with sound Principles of Life throughout this text. It is always mandatory to decipher the reality that divulges the negatives to be overcome.

This treatise is in fact an exposé in the spirit of "America Not So Beautiful." Every avenue that I followed I was confronted with confusion. The latter is a discouraging substandard Reality. So I decided to include avenues such as Culture, History and The Current State Of Our Democracy and proper leadership which to overturn the negative.

My sensitivity was challenged by the Reality and mannerisms of the existing culture. I concluded that it would be dishonest to turn away from this discovery of a massive state of the Decline of America. So I commenced researching vigorously for my new theme. I was truly amazed at the undercurrent of a splintered nation. A number of questions confronted me. How can this state of affairs be avoided by our elected free based Government? coping is unknown in our nation. The overall status has changed from peace and tranquility to one whereby it is shameful and discouraging to listen to the daily news. From a similar point of view, I concluded that the current low state of our nation is a detriment to longevity, peace and harmony for all of us. The fact that our nation is so splintered caused me to develop a strong desire to analyze the many negatives. I discovered an environment overcome by massive failings and negative social matters of all varieties.

Here, again, is a listing of unsavory aspects of the "Facial Hair and Cleavage Culture."

Samplings Of Cultural Problems

Again, what is wrong with our "Facial Hair and Cleavage Culture"? The list goes on and on, but for starters:

1. Thumping Drums Instead of Sweet and Soothing Music

At the most benign level, perhaps, we have public music. Music offers a particularly advantageous means to help all of society to cope, by relaxing, calming down, and feeling enveloped in harmony. This was also the goal of ballroom dancing. But since the 1950s, from Elvis Presley and the Beatles to Gangster Rap, it's used more to stimulate everyone within listening range. If you are not in danger of falling asleep, being over-stimulated all the time is exhausting, causes tension, and ends up creating an ongoing sense of stress even if you were calm before. All negative. But, like drugs, this cheap stimulation seems to appeal to an audience that never takes time to reflect on what is good and productive. And rather than being the most benign, perhaps this background is, in fact, a very strong influence on people's conduct.

2. Tie in violent, loud, shocking videogames and movies where the action makes no sense but everything is designed to get your heart pumping. Now, try to have a rational thought. Try to focus on what your partner is saying, and evaluate how to respond in accordance with the values you've chosen. You can't, can you? Are we being inundated in this environment intentionally?

3. Fake Advertising

Automobiles, like mot things these days, are not sold anymore on the true value of the product. Commercials are based on fantasy, showing high-speed driving on mountain roads, like a video game or movie – again, just cheap over-stimulation that prevents rational analysis of the product being presented.

4. Fake Politics

If you watch the mass media news, you'll be convinced that US politics have turned sharply and almost unanimously left. Yet the country voted for Trump, against the so-called liberal agenda which is, in fact, not what it claims to be. "Social Justice Warriors" are not promoting justice but endless hand-outs. They are confusing boundless illegal migration and bottomless social-support programs, to be paid for by the working populace through taxes, with voluntary charity and good works. They have not "done the numbers" and have no realistic way to pay for what they demand. Misunderstanding, rancor, lies, and all types of disgusting commentary turn off a large percentage of voters.

Then, it turns out very often that there is nothing in common between what candidates say and what they do, or even try to do, after being elected. So voters understand that they have no way to properly decide which candidate to vote for. Congress has been called the swamp which must be drained. I recommend that the status be changed to the Sewer.

5. Terrorism and Militarization

Terrorists are still being used worldwide to intimidate citizens and governments. No one knows where the next incident may be planned or by whom. At the same time, in our own streets, SWAT teams raid homes, sometimes the wrong ones; and the local police and Homeland Security headquarters display tanks and personnel carriers as if we were already living through World War III. People are constantly warned that we live in danger; "if you see something, report it." Yet another pressure on the populace.

6. Sexual Harassment

Sexual abuse seems to have penetrated our society from young people's sports and scouts groups to religious organizations. Hollywood executives and members of Government are also major offenders. In the case of Government it has been published that Congress has a secret fund where millions of dollars have been made available to help officials avoid victim complaints. This is not a sign of a healthy society.

7. Values

Your value inventory is very personal and explains your personality. The majority of people do not recognize this. If you ask a hundred people: Can you describe your value system? I doubt if you would even get 5 answers. If you pause and examine your value system in use you may find that you are frequently incorrect in your selection. This conscious recognition of reality is a positive activity and helps you behave in a more accurate response. Additionally it is a conscious concern regarding the perpetuation of your self-esteem.

8. Self-esteem

This characteristic is how you feel about yourself, which in term is highly dependent on your value system. It is difficult for people to hold to their self-esteem if they do not think through who they are and consciously select, and stick to, a set of positive values. When the surrounding environment is constantly pumping noise and stress and violence, it is particularly important to have a strong sense of yourself and be able to hold onto what is important.

Seventy-five years ago, America was a different country entirely. Correctness, righteous and harmonious behavior leading to peace and tranquility were habits broadly held among the population, and these values were encouraged throughout the culture. I argue that America the Ugly is now in effect and must be vanquished. Additionally, there is a great quantity of day to day current unsavory behavior to be studied that speaks for itself in its exposure.

In years gone by, the American dream was the goal of life. America was serene, with an established set of values regulating behavior. All of these factors are no longer in existence at the previous level. Occasionally someone will mention the notion of values. Based on Reality, only a minor percentage of citizens have established their lives to be on the path to the American Dream. That represents a severe alteration to our culture.

While I was putting together this book, I pondered how to cope with all of my findings. I wanted to describe the problem with integrity and in the absence of bias. In order to do so I have gone to great lengths to collect data and elements of Reality that are not easily recognizable in our environment. A great number of changes in the American culture are reported, with commentary leading to confusion.

At 95 years young, in advanced age, I enjoy the same level of activity and objectives of previous life without change. I am active in our government and proud to say that I am a member of The Presidential Advisory Board. I have my family constantly around me, indicating their love and respect for my history and my experiences. I feel a great responsibility to assist the unfortunate and therefore charity is an important influence in my life. The role of a senior person is to be one who provides his family and associates with a positive value system that helps himself and all those he interacts with.

Coping Enlightnement

1. Reality.

We have discussed the issue of Reality as Coping step number one. Reality is the way things really are and the first question becomes "What is the issue that needs to be clarified by discovering the reality for coping" which in this case is "The Facial Hair and Cleavage Culture. Select the basic data with full consideration of this issue as above. The warning herein lies in the word BIAS which unfortunately causes you to modify the pure findings of reality with predispositions that are improper.

2. Personal Awareness.

My very simple definition of this issue is as follows. If you don't See it or Hear it it never happens. This definition suggests a need for high level awareness to deal with the entire subject of Coping. In addition it is also suggested that Common Sense be included to the two previous senses of Hearing and Seeing. If you are half asleep while ignoring this warning you are on the wrong path.

3. Values

Everyone has a value system. Unfortunately it is not an awareness issue. So therefore it is highly recommended that the issue of your value system is fully understood. One important value is honesty. It is possible that while examining a culture there are individual situations that do not pass this test. Therefore they must be excluded totally. For example there were 56 million voters for Hillary with her questionable resume. Consequently voting for her as an issue that ignores ones values is a compromise of your self-esteem.

4. Total Coverage

At this point it is necessary to establish a relationship with yourself and the data. For example you have determined that "The Facial Hair and Cleavage Culture" is your subject of analysis. In this case it is clear that most of the problems of this culture are beyond the individual's ability to eliminate. This reality is most critical, since it allows you to recognize the problem in its pure terms. As an issue that is beyond the individual, you need to put it aside. You should develop an attitude that allows you to find peace and happiness while maintaining a realistic view of the culture in which we are immersed. So therefore annex Robinson's Law, "Think up front and live easy." Translated, it means that in dealing with issues that you have clarified, and where you have fully established the Reality, you then move to a review of the entire proposition with a high level of Personal Awareness, while seeing and hearing allow you to achieve "living easy."

5. Final Conclusion

In simplified terminology, step by step, we have clarified Coping with the culture in generalized terms as follows. Each step is uncomplicated and can be easily comprehended and applied, allowing the individual to achieve sufficient comprehension of an issue that may have been cloudy before. So Cope according to the formula and arrive at peace and happiness, while the state of our culture is recognized, understood and sensibly evaluated.

An Appropriate Fable

Many years ago there was an Indian Tribe in America in which their tribal name was unknown. It is interesting to note that the name of the chief was Sehawaya. He was treated with the great sense of reverence and was loved by his tribe. Other chiefs came to him for advice and he lived a life of quietude. Nobody could estimate his age. His name was revered over the entire western part of the new United States territory. He was the closest thing to a living deity and his disciples treated him accordingly.

Chief Sehawaya was frequently asked where did his name originate but without success. His fame multiplied while his name became a curiosity beyond expectation. After years of avoiding the question he became ill and was desirous of explaining the origin of his name. Accordingly he told the following story. Many years ago the Europeans came to his land. They seemed to be a happy, powerful and learned people with a special God. The chief Sehawaya further commented that his father selected the name for him when he was born. His reasoning came from his observation that the Europeans used the name Sehawaya as a greeting of power to each other.

Therefore he soon concluded that this power must be given to his son the new chief. Consequently naming the new child as Sehawaya. He wished to give his son the power of the Europeans. Yet when the son finally became chief he was not totally aware of the true meaning. However young Sehawaya became the chief and followed in his father's footsteps.

He noticed that there was love and friendship between the Europeans as they said the secret word. He did notice however that there was a high state of comradery among the Europeans. It apparently was derived from the power word Sehawaya. One day a priest came to the tribe to teach the religion of God. After several weeks he became very much aware of the special name Sehawaya. After considerable study he decided to explain the mystery as follows.

He said that when the European men used that name to each other, they were truly involved in expressing a litany of human values as follows:

> Truth, Love, Patriot, Honesty, Concern for others, Positive, Cooperation,
> Courtesy, Respect, Sympathy, Health, God, Kindness, Happiness, peace,
> Friendship, Accomplished, Motivation, Leadership, Reality Orientation.

The priest said that the word Sehawaya activated many desirable values among people and that he witnessed this favorable reaction among the Europeans when they said to each other Sehawaya. However the priest was a very intelligent man and immediately explained the mystery as follows. He said that the word Sehawaya is a derivative by the Indian vernacular and what they heard was immediately converted by the Indian mode of speech. When in truth the Europeans were speaking in English, the Indians heard the word Sehawaya. The Priest was able to decipher this matter. In English the words that they were saying to each other were: "So, how are you?"

In addition, that query activated a series of Codes of Behavior that are listed above in various combinations, which immediately elicited an enthusiastic response from the receiver. So in the light of the poignant message of chief Sehawaya and in closing the final chapter of our book, I wish to also bring attention to the

English meaning and associated values while with pride offering to my readers: SEHAWAYA.

Printed in the United States
By Bookmasters